The Practical Guide to Business Process Reengineering Using IDEF0

The Practical Guide to Business Process Reengineering Using IDEF0

Clarence G. Feldmann

Foreword by John V. Tieso

Dorset House Publishing
353 West 12th Street
New York, New York 10014

Library of Congress Cataloging-in-Publication Data

Feldmann, Clarence G.
    The practical guide to business process reengineering using IDEF0
  / Clarence G. Feldmann ;   foreword by John V. Tieso.
        p.   cm.
    Includes index.
    ISBN 0-932633-37-4 (softcover)
    1. Reengineering (Management)   2. Electronic data processing-
  -Structured techniques.   3. Business--Graphic methods.   I. Title.
    HD58.87.F45   1998
    658.4'063--dc21   98-20236
                                                                CIP

Cover Design: Jeff Faville, Faville Design
Cover Author Photograph: Joe Demb, Belmont, Massachusetts

Distributed in the English language in Singapore, the Philippines, and Southeast Asia by Toppan Co., Ltd., Singapore; in the English language in India, Bangladesh, Sri Lanka, Nepal, and Mauritius by Prism Books Pvt., Ltd., Bangalore, India; and in the English language in Japan by Toppan Co., Ltd., Tokyo, Japan.

Printed in the United States of America

Library of Congress Catalog Number: 98-20236

ISBN: 0-932633-37-4   12 11 10 9 8 7 6 5 4 3 2 1

Dedication

I dedicate this book to Douglas T. Ross, the father of SADT and IDEF0, with whom I worked for more than thirty years. The concepts presented here are his. I have tried to present his ideas as I have come to understand and apply them to the real world. I apologize to him for any misleading statements herein, or for dabbing on his canvas, as he used to put it.

GRAPHICS CREDITS

M any different graphics software packages were used to produce the figures in this book. Thus, the reader will see several variations in style
when reading the IDEF0 diagrams presented here. The use of a particular package to produce a specific form of IDEF0 diagram is not intended to imply
endorsement by the author. In most cases, the package used to develop an IDEF0
model was determined by the product used by the client for whom the model was
developed.

The following graphics packages were used to produce the diagrams in this
book, listed in alphabetical order of the package name:

Authormate, by Eclectic Solutions, Inc.
AutoCad, by Autodesk, Inc.
BPwin, by Logic Works, Inc.
Design/IDEF, by Meta Software, Inc.
SA/BPR, by Popkin Software and Systems, Inc.

ORRECTION
ease note that the Mechanism and Call arrows in Figure 4-1 (p. 56) and Figure 4-
(p. 71) should be reversed. Mechanisms are directed inward; Calls are directed
utward. We regret any confusion this error has caused.

CONTENTS

FIGURES &
TABLES

FOREWORD

O ver the past several years as I have traveled just about everywhere to discuss business reengineering, it has amazed me that most people think reengineering is a new phenomenon created by Mike Hammer. Some have been dumbfounded when I say how long it has been around and what it has accomplished during that time. I certainly give credit to Dr. Hammer's book for the publicity reengineering has received, but it is the unsung heroes that have made reengineering not just well known but successful.

One such hero is Clare Feldmann. He and I have been talking about and through his book for at least five years. Clare is one of those guys who prefers the background to the limelight. His years at SofTech with Doug Ross were the tough years as reengineering emerged into a modern method. More importantly, Clare was one of the pioneers in the belief that understanding processes and activities is the key to the application of technology to problems. This book shares with you many of his thoughts on how to effectively reengineer.

I will share one personal insight for you to bear in mind as you read the chapters that follow. Over the years, Clare and I have shared a number of opportunities, committees, boards, and so forth. At each, he takes very careful notes. In fact, more often than not, he converts them to IDEF0 activity diagrams and data diagrams. He has always claimed that he understands subjects better through models. By this time, he must have thousands of them. While I have no secret knowledge here, I will bet that a model exists for how to write a book. Ask him when you meet him.

Clare's love of models led to a deep understanding of how processes work. A lot of what we now say and do in reengineering efforts comes from that approach: Understand what you do now and look at what you can do to improve the process. When you model the reengineered process, it quickly becomes obvious how technology can help to further optimize the efficiency of the new process. All of this is quite logical—yet completely impossible to achieve without models. Clare's favorite technique is shown here—IDEF0—the integrated definition language that he helped create in the 1970's. That modeling technique captures information not obtainable otherwise. Understanding the controls on actions as well as the mechanisms that facilitate action is critical to creating business rules that clarify action.

Another benefit of Clare's effort is the timing. For those of us in Government, rapid change is upon us. The Information Technology Management Reform Act of 1996 now mandates that managers redesign processes before recommending information technology investments. In fact, this is a first step in bringing accountability to the hundreds of billions of dollars expended each and every year on technology in Government. With IDEF0, Clare shows managers a proven way to assure that those investments make sense.

Any time someone writes a book on reengineering, I cheer. Particularly so when the person writing the book has gotten his hands dirty with real work, in helping managers improve. We have too many volumes out there that discuss others' efforts, written by people who have never tackled a project themselves. Here you have a master who is describing his art—and the only charge for his services is the cost of the book. What a bargain!

If you only have time to read one book on the subject, this is it. Enjoy.

John V. Tieso
Former Deputy Director, Office of Functional Process Improvement
Office of the Assistant Secretary of Defense (OASD) for Command and Control, C3I
Arlington, Virginia

PREFACE

For many years, there has been a call for a comprehensive book on the IDEF0 method and its use in BPR. This book, written in answer to that call, is designed to introduce the method, its usage, and the benefits that can be achieved. It is also written to serve as a "do's and don'ts" document to identify the ways the method has been misused in the past and to specify ways to correct these misuses.

This book presents essential information about the IDEF0 method—its definition, basic rules of usage (including the standard language syntax and semantics as contained in the Federal Standard)—and lessons learned from many years of application in the real world. The examples depict actual commercial client and government agency models, from which names and proprietary information have been removed.

Who Should Read This Book

The material presented in this book is suitable for three categories of IDEF0 users:

- people who wish to explore the concepts and the application potential of IDEF0 for enterprise reengineering
- people who wish to determine how IDEF0 might be helpful to them in their systems analysis efforts

- people who have been introduced to IDEF0 concepts, and who wish to understand the theory behind the concepts so that they can use the method more effectively

The Department of Defense (DoD) Corporate Information Management (CIM) Office reports that more than 600,000 people worldwide fall into the third category, and one goal of this book is to provide meaningful assistance to such people during their IDEF0 analysis efforts.

After reading the book, a person should be familiar enough with IDEF0 to read and understand any IDEF0 model and should be able to understand how the method might be applied to enterprise or systems analysis and what goals and benefits are reasonable to expect from its application. However, to be considered an "author" of IDEF0 models, he must complete additional formal training and a brief apprenticeship period with an experienced IDEF0 author.[1]

Training courses in IDEF0 modeling are available from commercial vendors and at various universities, primarily in the United States;[2] SADT training courses are available worldwide.[3] In addition, there are more than a dozen good computer tools that support the IDEF0 method.

My hope is that this book will guide a new generation of modelers in producing the maximum benefit from IDEF0.

Winchester, Massachusetts   C.G.F.
April 1998

---

[1] Throughout this book, the male pronoun is used generically to include both males and females. Also, please note that in IDEF0 terminology, a *reader* is someone who knows the rules of the IDEF0 graphics and can therefore understand the diagrams. An *author* is someone who is a reader but who also is trained in creating IDEF0 models.

[2] For a list of registered vendors of courses and computer support tools for the IDEF family, write to Society for Enterprise Engineering, ATTN: Secretariat, c/o The Koop Foundation, 15825 Shady Grove Road, Suite 22, Rockville, MD 20850.

[3] SADT is the precursor to IDEF0. For more on SADT and the history of IDEF0, see Chapter 1 and Appendix C.

The Practical Guide to Business Process Reengineering Using IDEF0

Introduction
to the Method

CHAPTER 1

DEF0 is the most useful method of communication in my professional bag of tricks. This is a more radical statement than it may seem at first, considering that I count various programming languages (FORTRAN, Ada, and assembly code, for example), numerous software design methods (Yourdon, Parnas, and so on), multiple spreadsheet applications (such as Lotus and Excel), and *the English language itself* as other methods in this "bag." How can this be? It would seem that the English language would be the most valuable to me—it is, after all, my native language—but IDEF0 plays a unique role in my ability to communicate with people in my line of work.

Communication with IDEF0

Using IDEF0, I can communicate and validate my understanding of complex technical subjects of which I had little previous knowledge. It is the most effective way I know of to communicate with technical and nontechnical people, including management, and it plays a vital role in bridging the communication gap between these two groups. Prior to learning IDEF0, I would get mired in hundreds of pages of system specifications and even larger government requests for proposals (RFPs). Now, using the IDEF0 method, I can handle complexity without having to rely on the English language alone.

Overview of IDEF0 Syntax

The graphical elements of IDEF0 are very simple—just boxes and arrows. The boxes represent actions; the arrows represent interfaces between those actions. Figure 1-1 illustrates how IDEF0 syntax depicts a basic message in a simple IDEF0 diagram. The figure shows that the activity SELL PRODUCTS produces Cash, which is either deposited in a checking account or used to PAY BILLS.[1] Note that the Cash shown on the arrows represents physical cash, not information about the cash, as would be shown in a data flow diagram. IDEF0 diagrams present all manner of *things* on the data arrows—anything that is used by, is created by, or influences an activity.

Figure 1-2 shows the addition of control arrows to boxes 2 and 3 of the same diagram. The control arrow Money Owed represents outstanding bills and therefore controls how much may be deposited versus how much should be retained to pay bills. Figure 1-1 assumed that the bills are paid in cash—an assumption drawn from the "story" of the diagram. The addition in Figure 1-2 of the control arrow Checking Account Balance shows that bills may be paid by check.

Finally, Figure 1-3 shows the addition of IDEF0 mechanisms to the same diagram. We see that Bank is a mechanism required to make a deposit. Deposit Tickets are also needed, and the diagram indicates that these two mechanisms are used to deposit money in an account. The diagram also shows that both Deposit Tickets and Blank Checks are obtained from the Checkbook, and that Blank Checks are used to PAY BILLS, whereas Deposit Tickets are used to put Cash in the Bank.

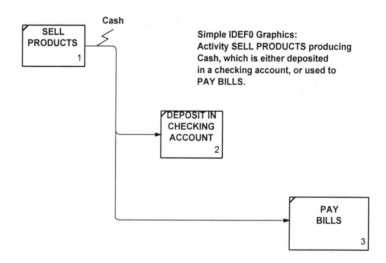

Figure 1-1: Simple Box and Arrow Graphics.

---

[1] As a style convention, in this paragraph I use initial caps to signify interfaces between actions, with the actions themselves set in small caps. For the sake of readability, I will use this convention only when unavoidable.

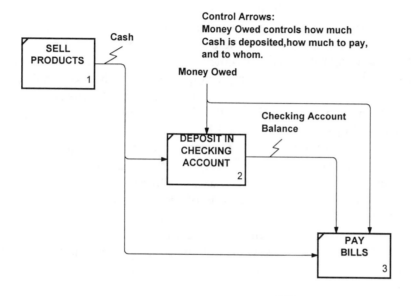

Figure 1-2: Simple Control Graphics.

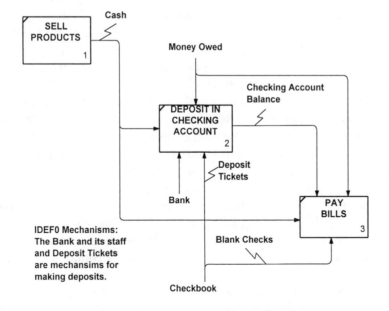

Figure 1-3: Simple Mechanism Syntax.

The simplicity of the graphics assumes that one of the major benefits of IDEF0—its ability to communicate to nontechnical and technical enterprise staff alike—will be upheld. Note how the four sides of an IDEF0 box support the reader's intuitive sense. Arrows entering the top of the box imply control (coming down on the activity and enforcing rules). Arrows entering the left side and producing data out the right side of the box imply an input-output relationship. Mechanism arrows coming into the bottom of the box imply a sense of support for the activity.

The communication power of IDEF0 provides an efficient and precise way to model real-world operations. Even without any training in IDEF0 syntax and semantics, anyone looking at these figures can understand the "story" being depicted. Attempts to elaborate on the IDEF0 syntax, such as adding AND/OR logic branches to arrows, different arrow syntax for different classes of arrows, and so on, all result in unacceptable complication of the diagrams and a failure to communicate effectively.

I discuss IDEF0 syntax and semantics in greater detail in Chapter 4. For now, to give the reader a feeling for the value of IDEF0 and to highlight its real contribution, I devote the next section to a brief history of the method.

Origins and History of IDEF0

As a graduate student at MIT in 1957, I worked under Douglas T. Ross at the Servomechanisms Laboratory (later to become the Electronic Systems Laboratory). Sometime before my arrival, Ross's lab had developed the first "numerically controlled machine tool" (a computer-controlled milling machine whose motions were controlled by a computer rather than by a machinist following a template) under a government-sponsored research contract with the Air Force Manufacturing Technology (ManTech) initiative to support the United States aerospace industry.

About the time I arrived, Doug Ross was starting a new project to develop a computer support system for programming this new milling machine, relieving programmers from developing lengthy and costly binary machine tool tapes by hand. Although I was not aware of the fact at the time, this was to be the first problem-oriented language in which the programmer wrote instructions to the computer in the user's technical language, rather than having to learn assembly code or FORTRAN (which was just being developed). The users were able to tell the computer, "Turn on the coolant," "Move in a straight line from point A to point B," "Retract the tool," and so on, instead of "If location A contains a 0, then set A equal to B." Clearly, weeks of work preparing a single tape could be reduced to a matter of minutes with this new computer language interpreter.

But this accomplishment is not the real issue here; the important point is to realize that this was a true breakthrough in communicating between one technical discipline and another—between the world of the computer programmer and the world of the machinist. Both were technically trained, but in different worlds, using different jargon, and having unique backgrounds and experiences that made them experts in their own diverse ways.

Now, turn the clock to the late 1960's. The numerical control industry had adopted the MIT system (called APT, for Automatically Programmed Tool) as a national and international programming standard. The same Air Force ManTech Office was attempting to help modernize and upgrade the aerospace industry's manufacturing capabilities in other ways. However, ManTech personnel were under heavy criticism for providing technology upgrade funds for a single aerospace manufacturer while being unable to provide equivalent support to all of the other aerospace companies.

Recalling their prior experience with APT, in which a coalition of aerospace companies cooperated with MIT to develop, distribute, and maintain the system, the Air Force once again turned to Doug Ross to suggest how it might develop support systems that could be used by an entire industry rather than a single company. Ross had long viewed the universe by looking at complex phenomena and applying the divide-and-conquer approach to decompose them repeatedly until each piece of the model was simple enough to understand and analyze. Consequently, Ross's answer to the Air Force's request was to develop an industry-wide model of how aerospace products are built and then to develop support systems that could be used by all (an open-system concept similar to that used today to build printers and monitors to be plug compatible with products from other personal computer manufacturers).

Ross's idea was accepted by the Air Force, and the Air Force Computer Aided Manufacturing (AFCAM) program was funded. This initial experiment was conducted in Seattle at Boeing, the company selected as representative of all aerospace operations. However, because the conglomeration of aerospace companies would only accept the result if developed by a coalition of the entire industry, it was not until 1978 that an industry-wide model was developed using Ross's modeling concept, and the Integrated Computer Aided Manufacturing (ICAM) contract was awarded to SofTech, Inc. (the company Ross had founded after leaving MIT).

An Early Opportunity

During the five years preceding the award of the ICAM contract, Ross's modeling method was applied to a commercial effort in a very different technical field, that of telecommunications. At that time, International Telegram and Telegraph Company (ITT) was developing specifications for the so-called Telephone System of the Future, which included call waiting, call transferring, and many of the other features that we take for granted today. ITT had a large specification effort going on in Europe for the new system, and the project was behind schedule. Experts from five countries were developing the specification, and they had reached an impasse. Documents in English, German, Spanish, French, and Italian sat on shelves in the ITT headquarters in Paris, and no one could determine whether information for different parts of the specification was complete, accurate, or compatible.

The solution was to reanalyze the subject using Ross's graphical modeling "language." The goal of the project was to identify elements missing from the specification and errors in the logic while analyzing the completeness and compatibility of the various components. A secondary goal was to provide a communication baseline between all parties. Because the job was too big for one small group of analysts, training courses were given throughout Europe to teach ITT staff how to do the modeling.

The ITT effort successfully pointed out problems in the existing specification (for example, where one group erroneously assumed that a second group was responsible for a portion of the analysis), and analysts from all five countries were able to communicate technical concepts and coordinate the interfaces between their parts of the planned system. Software specifications were written for portions of the renewed effort that was to follow. The Ross modeling method proved itself undeniably effective.

A Good Name

Another significant event took place at ITT's Paris headquarters during that same period. The manager of the ITT effort, Don Combelic, recognized the inherent usefulness of Ross's approach, and he decided that the modeling method needed a good name. He described the method as a structured analysis and design technique, and coined the term SADT. His intention was to show that the method was useful not only for analysis, but also for design, and he pointed out that the most important and innovative feature of the method was *traceability*—the ability to trace each user function back to the design element that implements that feature. Thus, using a mechanism arrow syntax, each user function was *traceable* to an element of the software, and no software element would be included that had no purpose from the user's perspective. This was a major advantage in ensuring complete and accurate communication between the nontechnical user community and the technical hardware or software development community.

Combelic required that the principles behind SADT modeling be documented (see the Seven Basic Principles, in Chapter 3), and also insisted that quality assurance issues be addressed, asking for specific methods for judging model quality.

By 1978, as mentioned earlier, the AFCAM effort in the United States was refunded and called ICAM, and a coalition of aerospace companies began developing the industry model of how they worked. They discovered that one company's product "breakback" structure was similar to a second company's "breakdown" structure, and that both were specialized forms of the common manufacturing document called a bill of materials. The model showed how these key elements were used and communicated during different parts of the manufacturing process, thus providing a greater level of understanding and management control. A follow-on project was then started to perform a similar analysis on the design portion of the aerospace operation, which complemented the manufacturing portion just completed.

A Series of Methods

By 1981, the Air Force recognized the usefulness of the modeling method and requested a formal Air Force version. The ManTech Office in the Air Force's Materials Laboratory expanded the concept to include a series of IDEF methods, naming the function-analysis portion of SADT that they found most useful "IDEF0."[2] A second method, named IDEF1, was developed for analyzing data and building databases.[3]

The acronym IDEF (*ICAM Definition*) describes a series of methods for developing ManTech products and integrating them into the daily operations of an enterprise. By decree, all IDEF methods are in the public domain, are freely available for use without any proprietary rights or licensing requirements, and may be used to define and integrate ManTech products. To date, three IDEF methods are supported by the Air Force and by United States industry; eleven additional methods are in some stage of research or development.

The full IDEF set (IDEF0, IDEF1, IDEF3) was designed to support systems analysis, where a "system" may be a computer system, a noncomputerized process, or an entire enterprise. Because IDEF0 by itself had demonstrated the ability to handle an enterprise's comprehensive scope and complexity, it was the first of the set of IDEFs to be applied to large enterprise analysis. IDEF proponents called IDEF0 a "methodology" because of its comprehensive nature, intending the term to signify that IDEF0 includes procedures for specifying its application and for accomplishing specific goals, and to convey that it was more than a mere technique or language. This use of the term "methodology" has become widespread among the IDEF user community, but I prefer to use the word "method" to describe IDEF0. My reasoning is that, strictly speaking, adding the suffix "ology" denotes "a study of," making a methodology a meta-view of methods. To me, methodologies consist of ways for describing and defining methods, which is not

---

[2] For a more detailed discussion of the history of and relationships between SADT, IDEF0, and IDEF1X, see Appendices C and D.

[3] IDEF3, a process analysis technique, has also been added; IDEF2 (using a simulation analysis approach) is not yet a formal member of the IDEF family.

the usage of the term adopted by the IDEF project. Rather than quibble over terminology, I use the word "method" to describe elements of the IDEF0 approach.

The division of the analysis phase into function (IDEF0) and data (IDEF1) took place during the ICAM program, and had the unfortunate side effect of causing camps to form among the analysts. The database camp viewed the world as a giant database, and argued that the only way efficient computer systems could be developed was if everyone adopted this viewpoint. The functional analysis camp insisted that data are useless unless one can see their functional purpose. This debate continues today, but may be swallowed up by the object-oriented approach, in which both function and data are combined into "objects."

Armed with these observations, we can now look more closely at the development of IDEF0 to see how the IDEF0 enterprise analysis approach is designed to satisfy the needs demonstrated by the ICAM and ITT experiences.

Elements of IDEF0

The IDEF0 method is comprised of three major elements based on the use of developing and using a model of the real world. The three elements of IDEF0 are *concepts, language,* and *pragmatics.*[4] This book describes IDEF0 in terms of these three distinct aspects, and shows students of the method that the maximum benefit from IDEF0 comes from understanding and using all three elements.

The *concepts* are at the foundation of IDEF0. They are ideas that the user of the method should believe in and adhere to if the rest of the approach is to make logical sense. These concepts are defined as the seven basic principles of IDEF0, and are presented in Chapter 3. They answer *why* one approach is used over another in the application of IDEF0, and they provide the experienced analyst with the rationale for following the rules, including when to bend them and when strict adherence is important.

The *language* of IDEF0 is the analyst's means of describing the activities of an enterprise. The language is written in graphical box-and-arrow notation on diagram forms that are structured to produce IDEF0 models. The language is used to convey meaning between the analysts, readers, enterprise management and staff, and others.

The *pragmatics* of IDEF0 provide the engineering procedures for using IDEF0. In many cases, the pragmatics are so closely tied to the concepts and language that they are inseparable, and analysts who have attempted to use IDEF0 without employing them typically have been unsuccessful. (When I present the most com-

---

[4] The word "pragmatics" was first used by Doug Ross to describe the key procedural aspect of the method, and is the word used by all IDEF modelers to describe practice and procedures.

mon misuses of IDEF0, later in this book, I show the kinds of problems that can occur if the pragmatics are not followed.[5])

To be effective, the IDEF0 method must be able to handle complexity. Therefore, behind the concepts, language, and pragmatics lies a basic principle: Divide and conquer. This principle assumes that any amount of complexity can be handled if it is broken down into small enough pieces, so long as the pieces are rigorously linked. This process has long been used in manufacturing. For example, in the aerospace industry, a modern aircraft includes more than three million individual parts. To understand this level of complexity, a designer breaks down the aircraft into its hydraulic system, its electrical system, and so on. So long as these individual parts work correctly and are integrated into the overall system, the aircraft's complexity is not a major problem.

Doug Ross stated the divide-and-conquer principle as an axiom:

> EVERYTHING WORTH SAYING ABOUT
> ANYTHING WORTH SAYING SOMETHING ABOUT
> CAN BE SAID WITH SIX OR FEWER PIECES.

Applying this principle to the modeling of systems, we begin an IDEF0 model with a high-level, single activity that represents the whole system. Breaking this into six or fewer pieces results in a diagram containing six or fewer activities and their interfaces. Each of these activities is then broken down into six or fewer sub-activities on decomposition diagrams.[6] This process is repeated until sufficient detail is presented to satisfy the purpose of the model.

---

[5] It is informative to note that during the development of the FIPS (Federal Information Processing Standard) for IDEF0 (FIPS 183), there was a lengthy discussion with the National Institute of Standards and Technology (NIST) about the inclusion of a pragmatics section in the Federal Standard. The authors were apparently not familiar with standards that included a pragmatics section. Because of this, and because of the foreseen difficulty with creating such a section of the standard, the IDEF0 pragmatics were not included in the "Normative" (required) section of FIPS 183, but were relegated to an "Informative" appendix. This appendix may or may not be referenced when determining if a specific use of IDEF0 does or does not comply with the FIPS 183 standard, as the user of the standard wishes.

It is also interesting to compare the IDEF0 FIPS with that of Ada, FORTRAN, and other existing standards. Here, the definition of the language syntax and semantics are included in the standard, but there is no mention of how to use the method. Similarly, the developers of the IDEF1X FIPS (FIPS 184) did not find a need for a pragmatics section, claiming that it did not matter how users developed the IDEF1X data model so long as the resulting graphics obeyed the standard syntax and semantics.

[6] The word "decomposition" conveys the form of breakdown used in IDEF0. An activity is decomposed into the elements that comprise it (as opposed to applying it in different environments, using it at different time phases, and so forth).

Following the divide-and-conquer principle thus results in a gradual exposition of detail as each activity decomposition diagram is studied by the reader. Each activity box on a diagram represents a well-defined context that sets the scope of the decomposition. This is a key in the communication power of the IDEF0 models, since the reader may study any aspect of the modeled system and explore finer detail about an activity of his choice.

Use of IDEF0 with Other Methods and Tools

Despite the mass of evidence reflecting successful IDEF0 application, the method still has not been widely accepted. In my view, there are two basic reasons for this: misuse and misconception.

Misuse of the method has been the focus of panel sessions at several IDEF Users Group conferences and is, in fact, such an important topic that I devote a whole chapter to the do's and don'ts. Chapter 6 also presents specific examples of the misuse of IDEF0 and describes ways to correct the problems. A discussion of the major misconceptions is presented below.

Misconceptions about IDEF0 abound. Some stem from the origins of the method with the Air Force's ICAM program. Key misconceptions concern the scope and topics that can be modeled, IDEF0's role in the system development life cycle, its ability to be used in conjunction with other methods, IDEF0's use with CASE (computer-aided software engineering) and other analysis and development tools, IDEF0's application to systems analysis, and finally, the belief that an analyst can create useful models with no IDEF0 authorship training or apprenticeship period. The following sections address these key issues in terms of IDEF0's relationship with various aspects of system development.

IDEF0 and Scope of Application

I'm often asked the question: "To what types of problems can IDEF0 be applied?" People think that since IDEF0 was developed as a means of depicting manufacturing processes, IDEF0's scope must be limited to manufacturing process models. This is not the case: The theoretical basis of IDEF0 is that it can be used to model any system comprised of *things* and *happenings*. This is a very broad scope; it is difficult to think of any subject to be modeled that contains no action or has no things to act on. Therefore, IDEF0 is perfectly applicable to such topics as strategic planning, project planning, shop floor process modeling, computer-/manual/hybrid systems design, and—of course—to business process reengineering.

Other frequently asked questions are: "Can IDEF0 depict parallel processes?" and "How is an IDEF0 diagram different from a flow chart or a data flow diagram?" Both questions show a lack of understanding about basic IDEF0 scope.

An IDEF0 model is made up of a set of IDEF0 diagrams that depict *constraint*, not *flow*. Each function box on an IDEF0 diagram depicts the function described by the verb phrase written in the box whose further detail may be found on decomposition diagrams. The arrows shown entering and leaving the boxes depict things that are *needed* by or *produced* by the function. Whenever sufficient inputs and controls are available on the arrows, a box is considered to activate and produce output. The availability of this output may, in turn, cause one or more other functions to activate, since the availability of some input or control that was causing them to be inactive is not available on the arrow.

Thus, any or all boxes may be active, depending on the availability of their inputs and controls. In fact, this precisely matches the real world, which was a goal of the modeling effort. If the user wishes to apply IDEF0 to model the internal operation of a computer software system that runs on a sequential processor, then he must add control arrows to the IDEF0 model that will cause the processor to activate in a sequential manner.

Returning to the questions posed above, we now see answers: "Yes, IDEF0 does handle sequential processing." "No, IDEF0 is not a flow chart, since it does not prescribe a sequence of operation." Furthermore, since the IDEF0 model displays all constraints on each function, "IDEF0 is a constraint model, not a flow model."

The origins of IDEF0 also might make one believe that it should only be applied to very large systems analysis and design efforts. Clearly, these large-scale efforts were what IDEF0 was first used to accomplish (in them, everyone could see that a very large system would be impossible to describe in detail without some better means than text or existing computer system design charts). Traditional approaches did partially accomplish the goal: For example, the block diagram method with text is one step in the right direction but shows only the major elements without defining what the connecting lines mean and what information, materials, and paperwork pass between the blocks. Flow charts are also helpful, but a large system requires a very large chart (the largest such chart I have run across was 72 feet long). Even with a large chart, the important information flows and other aspects are not included in flow chart graphics.

These observations show that IDEF0 is appropriate for handling large systems, but what about its usefulness for small systems? Isn't using IDEF0 to analyze or design small systems the equivalent of driving a thumbtack with a sledgehammer? It is true that small systems are more easily understood, and that a text, block diagram, or flow chart approach might suffice. However, once IDEF0 has been learned and become part of an analyst's repertoire, he generally finds that IDEF0 is quicker and more easily used to define even small problems, since it provides such a natural and communicational means of expressing a system's elements and their dynamics.

IDEF0 and the System Development Life Cycle

The next misconception about IDEF0 is that, because there already are many well-known and widely used modeling methods, it is not needed. Surveys constantly compare IDEF0 with modeling methods such as Yourdon, Gane and Sarson, and object-oriented design. This is like comparing apples and oranges—which is better?

IDEF0 is the only method on this list that was originally intended for the early problem-definition stages. All of the others assume a well-defined problem, and then focus on developing a solution. Recent emphasis on business process reengineering and on the now-recognized need to provide a modeling method for the problem-definition phases preceding the development phase have fostered the use of IDEF methods. This is not to say that these other methods cannot be used for enterprise analysis and problem definition (especially useful are object-oriented methods), but the vast body of experience is clearly with IDEF0. Recently, when members of the National Institute of Standards and Technology (NIST) began development of a Federal Information Processing Standard (FIPS) for IDEF0, they published a call in the Federal Register for other public domain methods in the same category as IDEF0, and none was identified.

A key IDEF0 characteristic is that it deals with all aspects of a system (hardware, people, resources, raw materials, information, forms, and procedures), whereas these other methods typically handle one aspect only—information. It is true that information about the hardware, people, and resources is what is important for computer processing systems, but information processing ultimately is aimed at a solution, not at defining the problem. Many people believe that the major benefit of an IDEF0 analysis is the development of a computer system, but often equally significant benefits are non-computer-oriented, such as company reorganization, simplified procedures, better use of staff, and sharing of resources.

The most glaring weakness in other problem-definition methods is their inability to communicate complex concepts quickly and to nontechnical staff. The simple box-and-arrow syntax of IDEF0 easily communicates information between software-oriented staff, management, support staff, and all others who need to understand the system and verify a model's accuracy.

IDEF0 and CASE

Typically, CASE technology is employed when management has determined what new computer systems are to be developed in support of an enterprise reengineering effort. Although CASE may be expanded at some date to include the systems analysis effort, the analysis role is not typically associated with CASE today.

Thus, modeling of the total enterprise and its support systems typically occurs prior to the employment of CASE technology. IDEF0 is used during the early planning effort to understand how the system now works (an AS-IS model) or is desired to work at some time in the future (a TO-BE model). It is most useful for identifying problem areas and for planning improvements. Once these improvements have been planned, a CASE tool may then be employed to specify and design a solution—commonly, a computer support system to automate one or more problem areas shown in the IDEF0 model.

IDEF0 and Systems Analysis

Early applications of the modeling method in the ITT and ICAM programs provided valuable lessons in the emerging field of systems analysis. The most basic lesson was that SADT and IDEF0 did provide computer scientists with the ability to analyze and communicate between all of the technical and nontechnical staff necessary to understand and build complex systems, but there were additional lessons:

Lesson 1:   *A typical IDEF0 diagram represents a considerably more concise presentation of information than text.* The ratio on the ITT and ICAM projects was between ten and fourteen pages of text for each page of IDEF0 model containing equivalent information.

Lesson 2:   *Only ten to fifteen percent of IDEF0 students possess the analytical talent to apply the method as originally intended.* The remainder of the class can become readers, can critique models, and can participate in implementing changes.

Lesson 3:   *If an IDEF0 model is well done, it looks simple and is easy to understand, which can make untrained modelers believe they don't need formal training or experience.* This is a serious problem that leads to the creation of bad models.

Lesson 4:   *The IDEF0 method is more than a language; it includes procedures for its application (the so-called pragmatics of the method).* One of these procedures, the "reader/author" critique cycle, is a key to developing useful models that are accurate, communicative, and complete (see Chapter 5, Pragmatics).

Lesson 5:   *The people-oriented considerations of running an IDEF0 modeling project are critical.* An egoless environment for development fosters a high-quality critique of draft model results.

Lesson 6:   *Depending on the technical background of the management, presentation of the IDEF0 model to top-level management may not be wise.* Other forms of presentation, all based on facts derived from the model, may be more appropriate (see Chapter 4).

Lesson 7:   *The development of a big-picture functional model should be tackled first, before any other form of analysis begins.* No matter how great the pressure from the computer community to forget the functional model and to *just get on with systems development,* management wants to see the big picture that only a top-down functional model can provide.

IDEF Methods and Object-Oriented Methods

The popularity of object-oriented analysis methods has caused speculation as to the future of IDEF methods. Research at NIST was recently conducted to determine what roles IDEF and the object-oriented methods will play in enterprise engineering efforts in the future. Early conclusions are that IDEF and object-oriented methods can work together, and that both are important to enterprise analysis efforts: Object models provide a means of formally analyzing an enterprise, whereas IDEF0 models provide process definition and a means of communication that is critical to enterprise engineering. There is reason to anticipate that a future melding of IDEF0 and object-oriented methods can be advantageous to both.

IDEF Models and Integration with Other Methods

Many other modeling and analysis methods exist. Many of these methods contain very helpful syntax for analyzing or designing specific types of processes. We need not use these other methods in isolation, but can achieve significantly greater benefit by integrating their graphics with IDEF0.

The following chapter explores IDEF0's unique applications to business process reengineering and the analysis of enterprises.

Using IDEF0 for Process Improvement

CHAPTER 2

In the commercial arena, Michael Hammer and Michael Champy have led the Business Process Reengineering movement in which companies revise their organizational and operating procedures to become *lean and mean.* In *Reengineering the Corporation,* Hammer and Champy focus on business processes, and advocate fundamental, radical, dramatic change (their three key words). The objective is to enable companies to survive in the competitive environment of the future.

Hammer and Champy's approach requires a strong management team with solid support. Furthermore, the members of this team must be able to think *inductively,* more than *deductively.* That is, the team must be able to "first recognize a powerful solution and then seek the problems it might solve."[1]

Though most commonly applied in the commercial arena, Hammer and Champy's approach has also taken root in the government arena—most specifically in the Department of Defense (DoD).[2] Motivated by the collapse of the Soviet Union and the need to downsize the military, the Bush Administration appointed

---

[1] See Michael Hammer and Michael Champy, *Reengineering the Corporation* (New York: HarperBusiness, 1993), p. 84.

[2] The actual jurisdiction of this work was under the Office of the Assistant Secretary of Defense for Command, Control, Communications and Intelligence (OASD/C3I). However, in this book, the distinction between OASD and DoD is not made, but the term DoD is used uniformly for both levels of reengineering effort.

Paul A. Strassmann Director of Defense Information and chartered him to accomplish a \$350 billion reduction in the DoD budget over a five-year period. The Corporate Information Management (CIM) organization was formed as the new agency responsible for this government downsizing effort.

Wanting the most effective nonproprietary method to accomplish his goal with minimum breakage,[3] Strassmann championed widespread use of IDEF0 by the DoD.

Use of IDEF0 in Support of BPR

The ICAM and ITT applications of SADT and IDEF0, described in the previous chapter, were early examples of Business Process Reengineering (BPR) enterprise analysis, although they weren't called that at the time. From those experiences, the following observations were made about the fundamental criteria for applying IDEF0 to support a successful reengineering effort:

> **Culture:** An enterprise usually consists of many cultures.[4] Each culture has a unique terminology or jargon that is key to understanding that culture. If the enterprise's cultures do not communicate well between each other, a communication gap can arise.
>
> **Communication:** The many different viewpoints of an enterprise need to be analyzed in order to understand, control, and change that enterprise effectively. The diverse cultures need to support each other and work together if the enterprise is to be successful. Support by one culture (for example, computer systems) requires an understanding of the needs of the foreign culture (for example, manufacturing). In addition, the support requirements must be communicated to management as well as between the staffs in both cultures if one culture is to effectively support another. To be able to control complexity, developers need to trace requirements from the user culture to solutions in the support culture.
>
> **Documentation:** How an enterprise operates is typically recorded only in the heads of the experts who operate that enterprise, not in company manuals. Documentation is essential.

---

[3] In this context, "breakage" is defined as time lost and expense incurred when attempting to implement a change.

[4] By my definition, a culture consists of people with similar training and backgrounds who work together to provide their unique enterprise contribution. Examples of such cultures are accountants, engineers, secretaries, machinists, and so on.

Graphics: Complexity can be understood if it is broken down into small enough pieces, with the interfaces between the pieces defined precisely. One-dimensional text-based descriptions are not adequate to convey an enterprise's complexity or to communicate requirements; two-dimensional graphics are needed. A graphics-based model of the elements of an enterprise can serve as an effective communication and planning baseline.

Procedures: The application of the modeling method must be governed by proven basic principles and concepts, as well as by orderly and controlled procedures (pragmatics), or the effort will not be successful. To develop the graphics-based model, the staff must participate in its development, validate the details, and buy into any changes that result from the analysis.

Model template: Many enterprises have more in common with other enterprises than they realize; often, a broadly applicable model of a class of enterprise can be reused to save time and budget.

After the early BPR applications on the ICAM and ITT programs, the IDEF0 method was used primarily by the aerospace industry and the Air Force to analyze and plan modernization efforts. However, its utility for reorganizing and improving the *total* enterprise was recognized but not capitalized on by the user community until the Department of Defense applied it in its own reorganization and downsizing.

Use of IDEF0 for Military Downsizing and Reorganization

The great potential of IDEF0 was articulated by Strassmann in his keynote presentation to the IDEF Users Group in Washington, D.C., in October, 1992. Speaking before more than four hundred government and industrial managers, Strassmann noted that the United States is moving "from an industrial civilization to an information civilization," and that while during the past two hundred years the nation had experienced an astounding productivity growth, progress had stagnated in the preceding decade. Tracing one cause of this stagnation to unreasonably large overhead costs, Strassmann observed that the overhead labor and managerial province had not been subject to the kind of "meticulous examination" that technology had experienced during the same decade. He noted further that personal taxes, which have been cited as a great burden at 35 to 40 percent, pale in comparison with the enormous burden American business bears in its overhead, which typically ranges from 40 to 80 percent. Strassmann reported his goal: to reduce the overhead and management costs of the "checkers, auditors, lawyers, coordinators, procedure writers. . . . The people who check the checkers are a tax upon it."

Strassmann advocated a form of BPR that is tailored to government needs and that fits into the DoD environment. Furthermore, he cited IDEF0 as the only analysis method that had achieved the record of success required for understanding and controlling an Information Age enterprise.

Instead of applying Hammer and Champy's concept of Business Process Reengineering—of fundamental, radical, dramatic change—the Department of Defense had to make use of existing or so-called legacy systems (to relocate personnel, for example) or to convert existing facilities for new purposes (for example, converting a military base into an airport or a prison). This involved an analysis of present operations (the AS-IS picture) before detailing the picture of future operations (the TO-BE picture).

Although some BPR proponents argue against analyzing the current enterprise, saying that we should strike out in new directions, the DoD could not afford this luxury to the extent that a commercial enterprise could. BPR proponents are right that we must not get stuck automating the old manual ways of running the operation, but it is essential that we see how the current operation can be evolved into the new operation. There must be a solid, inductively reasoned vision of the future operation that is not encumbered by old ways, but there also must be a *clear path from here to there*. That path depends on knowing precisely how the enterprise works now. However, this approach of modeling the current system has several inherent dangers:

- The analysis of the AS-IS picture may become bogged down and the objective inadvertently changed to one of automating the present operation.
- The enterprise may lack a strong leader to drive the development of the TO-BE operation, or there may not be a key cadre of managers and staff supporting the leader's effort, top down and bottom up.
- The enterprise reengineering process may not include enough tasks that can be performed by the large number of people involved in the reengineering project.

The reengineering process employed by the DoD required well-thought-out steps and stages, with carefully devised roles for all project members. IDEF0 models used in such a process must reflect the same inductive reasoning described by Hammer and Champy (for example, "IDEF0 is the method—now where can it best be used to accomplish the goals of the effort?").

IDEF0 is at the heart of the DoD's version of Business Process Reengineering. The DoD's BPR procedure, as originated by the CIM office, is an example of a well-defined method that prescribes specific models to be developed and provides a description of the use for each model once it is completed.

Although currently undergoing revision, the basic CIM process is summarized in Table 2-1. The eight steps in which use of the IDEF0 models is specifically pre-scribed are noted by a checkmark.

Table 2.1.
The DoD/CIM 25-Step BPR Process.

Phase I - Strategic Planning

Secure Commitment
Define Mission
✔ Develop Strategic Plan
Analyze Best Practices

Phase II - Business Planning

Develop Business Plan
✔ Document Current Processes
✔ Document the Functional Architecture
Initiate Functional Process Improvement (FPI) Project

Phase III - Process Analysis

✔ Revise AS-IS Activity Models
Revise AS-IS Data Models
Use Activity-Based Costing (ABC) for Cost Estimation
Analyze Cost/Best Practice
Make Recommendations

Phase IV - Process Design

✔ Develop TO-BE Initiative Package
✔ Develop TO-BE Activity & Data Models
✔ Revise TO-BE Package
Select Based on Economic Analysis
✔ Develop Detailed TO-BE
Develop Preliminary Functional Economic Analysis (FEA)
Develop TM and DM Plans
Develop FEA Decision Package

Phase V - Project Execution

Develop Project Action/Trans Plans
Make Executive Presentations
Execute FEA Package
Evaluate Results/Update Baseline

Benefits of Using IDEF0 Models for Enterprise Reengineering

Having worked on commercial BPR projects and having applied the DoD's BPR process for several years, I have seen substantial evidence of the benefits that IDEF0 brings to any reengineering effort. Overall, this positive feedback amounts to more than that received after similar use of SADT since its inception. Even still, at the completion of a BPR project, enterprise management typically asks: *What is the benefit of using IDEF0 when the information could have been obtained by interviewing the experts and identifying those things that need improvement?*

This is a reasonable question to ask: Is it worth the time and expense, including all of the training and paperwork? It is true that improvements in an enterprise can be specified in English, without any graphics, and simple improvements have indeed been defined and implemented using English only. However, the more complex the enterprise, the more far-reaching the effects of a change—and, the more complex the enterprise, the more the staff members must document their area of expertise and the more misunderstandings will arise in defining a change. There is a consensus today that the use of a graphical language approach such as IDEF0 reduces misunderstandings and facilitates the main objective: change control and planning.

Clearly, the software industry has been developing systems for a sufficiently long period that the effect of a graphical design language on the quality of the resulting system has been seen. Since the 1970's, when graphical design languages came into vogue, statistics show that computer systems designed with textual requirements and textual design alone contain more than twice the number of errors and oversights than comparable systems designed using a graphical language (any graphical language—it doesn't seem to make a difference which one is used).

The same effect should apply to the enterprise reengineering experience. Yes, the enterprise may be redesigned using only textual descriptions of the improvements, but that will result in considerably more breakage when the resulting change is implemented into daily enterprise operations. The effect is unavoidable, not because the staff implementing the change is not careful or sufficiently knowledgeable, but because the complexity of the operation and the impacts of the change are just not evident without a graphical model of the enterprise.

So far, this discussion of IDEF0 has focused on the graphical language alone. In itself, graphical expression is a major aid in enterprise reengineering, but the benefits can be further leveraged with a well-designed engineering discipline. Engineering methods verify the correctness and completeness of the facts portrayed by the model, and they examine a level of detail that usually resides only in the heads of the staff.

Taking into consideration Hammer and Champy's concept of inductive reasoning, as well as the twenty-five DoD/CIM steps for running a BPR project, let's look at how the IDEF0 method can be used to support BPR efforts. Properly used, an IDEF0 modeling effort uncovers and documents the processes of an enterprise in a more precise format and comprehensive scope than any other popular modeling method available today. For an AS-IS model, the IDEF0 reader/author critique procedure validates the correctness and completeness of the model's facts; for a TO-BE model, the method provides the planning staff with a means of defining improved processes and a way of gaining consensus and common understanding among the management of the enterprise.

An AS-IS IDEF0 model of an enterprise cannot help but uncover obvious improvements that are simple to implement and that provide an immediate return on investment, which often can justify the modeling expense by itself. The argument is that once management sees precisely how the enterprise actually operates, it finally has the needed information to tune the operation, rather than rely on the "everything is under control" picture painted by subordinates who do not want to make waves.

These improvements are the low hanging fruit, but are not the total of the benefits. To get the most return from an IDEF0 model, one must insure that the purpose for creating the model is well defined. The general rule is: Never create a model for the purpose of creating a model. To do so would indicate a lack of vision on the part of management. The obvious improvements resulting from developing the model will be achieved anyway; the project needs a more focused purpose. To achieve this, we write the purpose statement (required on the topmost diagram of the model) in the form, "This model will be used to . . ." By following this format, we assume that the purpose statement defines how the model will be used once it is completed. Note that the manager of the modeling project should thus relate the model's usage purpose to the project plan task structure.

The following sections further describe the benefits of the reader/author cycle, the workshop approach, and the AS-IS modeling process.

The Reader/Author Cycle and the Workshop Approach

Two major methods of gaining consensus and critiquing the content of an IDEF0 model are currently employed: the reader/author (R/A) cycle and the workshop. The R/A cycle is the original approach used on SADT projects, and the workshop is a subsequent approach developed by the DoD for reorganizing government enterprises.

Neither method is likely to be wholly successful: The R/A cycle may bog down if individual reviewers do not provide in-depth review on their own volition; the workshop sessions involve user experts in defining requirements, but they can be prohibitively expensive and may leave insufficient time for the IDEF0 author to perform the actual analysis.

In the second case, the IDEF0 author may spend 100 percent of his time documenting what the workshop attendees are describing, leaving him no time whatsoever to practice the skill for which he was trained—analysis of systems. The workshop format can force use of the IDEF0 language for documentation, not for analysis, a situation analogous to that in which an author is asked to write a book by committee. The resulting work lacks the insight of a single author and does not flow as smoothly as when the author is free to practice his trade without interference.

On the other hand, the single-author R/A cycle method has the disadvantage that important consulting-expert opinion might be missed, or that a thorough evaluation of the model might not be accomplished because busy people can't take the time to respond to a request for a written critique (as required by the R/A cycle). The danger is that consensus and buy-in by the management and staff may not be achieved.

A solution would be to combine the best of both methods into a new scheme that gives the author a chance to use his talents and yet achieves the enterprise consensus required for follow-through implementation. In this combined approach, the IDEF0 author would interview key management personnel to gain overview insight into the operation of the enterprise from management's perspective, and he would also hold workshops for the staff to define the actual process detail to make the model real and not just conjecture. The staff workshops would not be full-day information-gathering sessions, but would begin with half-day sessions and a strawman model developed by the author from prior interviews and documentation.[5] Since management would not be invited to the staff workshops, the staff would be free to modify the model to reflect reality.

This approach avoids the awkward and difficult job of trying to get the staff to provide the big picture of the enterprise—a critical modeling level that can only be developed from the perspective of top management. At present, the development of this part of the model in workshop mode with only the staff present meets with impatience and a "Why are we wasting our time with this? We need to get down to the details" attitude.

By attending half-day workshops rather than full-day sessions, staff members are not away from their daily duties for long periods of time and the cost due to work interruption is reduced—a clear benefit. Most important, half-day sessions give the IDEF0 author a chance to *think* about what he is analyzing and to apply

---

[5] A "strawman" is a draft created as a talking point for a group session. It is expected to include inaccuracies, but it serves to focus discussion on specifics rather than generalities.

his analysis skills—a critical element of the BPR workshop approach that is missing from the continuous session workshop approach practiced at so many sites.

Following the interview and workshop sessions, the author creates the model and writes the accompanying text (which, under present IDEF0 working rules, he must do *during the meeting*). The improvement opportunities are documented as part of the text that accompanies each diagram, thus focusing the reengineering effort on the findings of the modeling effort.

The major deliverable, or work product, of the BPR project consists of a set of precise, accurate, communicative improvements described in graphical and textual form. These improvements mirror the knowledge of the group that created and reviewed the AS-IS model and the farsightedness of the group that developed the TO-BE IDEF0 model. The remaining effort is to develop and follow through on the plans to implement the improvements, in an orderly fashion, and with minimum breakage to the enterprise's viability to function during the change-over period.

IDEF0 models are not created for the sake of creating models—they each have a well-defined purpose in the overall BPR effort. They represent a valuable language with which to express ideas to the critical personnel of the enterprise who themselves are involved with the planning and implementation of the change.

Consider, for example, an enterprise and its past attempts to manage change and implement improvements using text and the block diagram approach characteristic of structured analysis and data-oriented analysis. The traditional planning documentation is too verbose and difficult to follow. When changes are implemented, there is considerable breakage, and it takes a great deal of time and money to get things working smoothly again. From the human-factors perspective, implementation of the changes typically takes a strong management push. Buy-in by the staff is pursued, but the fortitude and persistence of management is the key factor in accomplishing the change.

By using IDEF0, one can better understand, communicate, and validate the proposed changes. The graphical language makes concepts easier to understand and communicate. The staff, who is familiar with the details, can evaluate the portion of the model it is most familiar with; management can study the higher-level diagrams to understand the big picture.

To sum up, then, the primary benefit of the use of IDEF0 for BPR is: *the ability to manage change*. This ability is the key to overcoming the chief roadblock to implementing BPR improvement, since effective change management results in lower cost and less breakage. If computer system design experience can be used as an analogous measuring stick, then approximately 50 percent of the errors and oversights should be avoided—a very significant cost- and time-saving benefit.[6]

---

[6] This section has provided a management-oriented discussion of benefits; for a *technical* discussion, see Chapter 3.

The AS-IS Model

Analysts are often asked: "What is the value of developing an AS-IS model? Why not just model the TO-BE picture of how we envision the improved enterprise?" The following brief stories illustrate the value of AS-IS modeling:

A large manufacturer attempted to implement a parts-tracking system to comply with a stringent new government requirement. After an investment of six million dollars and more than a year of development, the new system was ready to go online.

The enterprise soon discovered that there had been significant misunderstanding by the new system's developers regarding information currently being conveyed manually. The cause was the lack of in-depth understanding of the AS-IS picture of the manufacturing operation. In this case, a daily phone call passed important information between the scheduling staff and the shop floor, but because this key communication path was not documented in the company's manuals and because no AS-IS analysis had been performed, the passing of information was overlooked when the new computerized system was built. The system had to be scrapped.

Having learned a costly lesson, the manager of the new system development project became an IDEF0 convert and manager of the SADT/IDEF0 analysis organization, claiming that he would never again fall for the trap of building a new system with insufficient information about the AS-IS operation.

At another company, strategic planners welcomed the introduction of IDEF0, since they had been through what they considered to be the typical sequence of system-development events, as follows:

Step 1: Plan the introduction of a manufacturing process improvement effort, including a budget for AS-IS analysis.

Step 2: Buy equipment, experiment with the new process, and begin building pieces of the new system.

Step 3: Experience overruns, discover hidden costs, and reestimate the job's cost and schedule.

Step 4: Cut the budget for AS-IS analysis, and increase the implementation funds.

Step 5: Spend several times the AS-IS analysis's original budget patching and getting the improvement to work properly, with a typical one-year schedule slippage.

Step 6: Return to Step 1 with the next improvement idea.

In this second company, the IDEF0 method of developing an AS-IS model was applied to *one area only*, as an experiment to evaluate the value of the approach. As the model was developed, it was used to reveal several significant oversights in meetings with management. In addition, analysis of the AS-IS operation brought out several other simple improvements that were subsequently approved by management.

Unfortunately, the remaining budget for IDEF0 AS-IS analysis was soon required to cover the overruns in the other areas. The areas in the improvement project that were not using IDEF0 methods had grossly exceeded their budgets. The IDEF0-based experiment was terminated. Yet another company had fallen into the old trap! Again, the major problem was a lack of management support for the IDEF0 analysis.

Additional horror stories abound, but here are a few examples from my own experience that show the positive effect of using IDEF0. These cases present four different kinds of BPR improvement:

Case 1: using IDEF0 to facilitate needed information flow between accounting and project management
Case 2: using IDEF0 to reduce the cost of government proposal development
Case 3: using IDEF0 to analyze poor performance of a company's field office
Case 4: using IDEF0 to introduce new business process concepts, such as Total Quality Management and agile manufacturing

Case 1: Facilitate Information Flow

The problem, as stated to enterprise management, was that project expenses were not being controlled properly. Examples of cost overruns were common, and project managers blamed this on the lateness and inaccuracy of project cost reports provided by the enterprise's accounting department. In addition, small contracts frequently encountered additional costs several months after the contract was closed, due to late processing of expenses. This resulted in embarrassing calls to customers to ask them to make unexpected additional payments, or in costly absorption of these expenses by the enterprise.

Clearly, the accounting department's processing of expenses had to be faster and the accuracy of the records improved. To pin down the causes of the problem and to determine which changes would be effective, we analyzed the enterprise in the area of the accounting department's processes. The complete model developed as part of this analysis is presented in Appendix B (Sample Models). As an illustration, a diagram that identifies one source of delay is reproduced here.

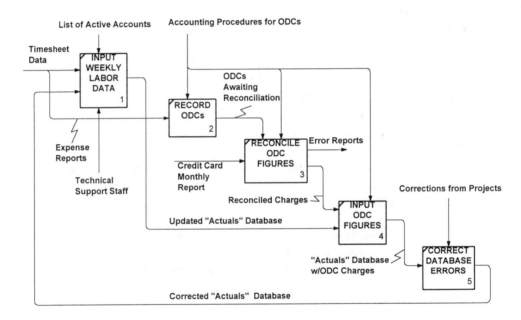

Figure 2-1: Keep Contract "Actuals" Records.

In the diagram, boxes 2, 3, and 4 show the process of handling the expense reports (in accounting terms, Other Direct Charges or ODCs) turned in by the project staff. When an Expense Report is turned in (see box 2, input 1), the data are recorded in the company's accounting system. No reports on expenses are provided to the project manager until actual payment is made for all items on the expense report, including air fares (this policy is the result of a DoD regulation designed to reduce efforts on corrections when trips are changed). Payment is therefore triggered by the receipt of the invoice for air fares on the monthly corporate credit-card account (see box 3, input 1). This notice may be received by the accounting department more than two months following the actual trip, due to billing cycles at the credit-card company. If discrepancies are encountered, further delays may be incurred while accounting staff members reconcile the data (see boxes 3). Finally, the ODC figures are entered into the company accounting system (see box 4). The information is then reported to the project manager in the next monthly contract accounting report, which may add nearly another full month to the delay.

The improvement sought by the IDEF0 analysis was to reduce or eliminate the delays. This could be done by instigating an encumbrance accounting report to send to the project manager (a report generated as soon as the trip expense report is received at box 2), by eliminating the credit-card company billing service and performing this task in-house, or by processing air fares separately from other ODCs, since these will not change after the trip has occurred.

The TO-BE improvement selected was development of an encumbrance system, since any change in the contract with the credit-card company would have had a large ripple effect on other aspects of the company's accounting process. Furthermore, the use of an encumbrance system had many other beneficial side effects, such as providing more timely financial information in other areas (not shown). The investigation into which improvement to select involved an in-depth analysis of the overall effect of each of the possible approaches, including whether a significant financial return on investment (ROI) would offset the cost of developing and converting to the new in-house system.

Case 2: Reduce Costs

The cost of developing government proposals has risen staggeringly over the past twenty years. Proposals now often exceed a thousand pages, and sheer volume gives rise to a considerable amount of waste in the proposal development effort. At one company we studied, these costs had increased overhead to the point where the enterprise was having difficulty remaining competitive.

As was done in Case 1 with the problem of improving accounting department cost reporting, we analyzed one aspect of the enterprise to identify how the proposal development process could be improved. Once a model of the marketing area had been decomposed to a fine level of detail, analysts interviewed the proposal development staff to solicit suggestions for improvement. The results of the interview were documented using the diagrams of the model to show specifically how the proposal development process would be run in the future. This information was then used to develop a TO-BE model of this area.

When modeling the proposal preparation process, the IDEF0 author noted that each field office organized the proposal team differently. Some proposals included a coalition of subcontractors, whose contributions to the overall proposal were handled like a small proposal to the prime contractor. Whether or not there were subcontractors, the entire team typically met to discuss overall strategy and plan key proposal elements, based on the award factors presented in the government's RFP. Figure 2-2 presents the resulting diagram: "Organize & Manage the Effort."

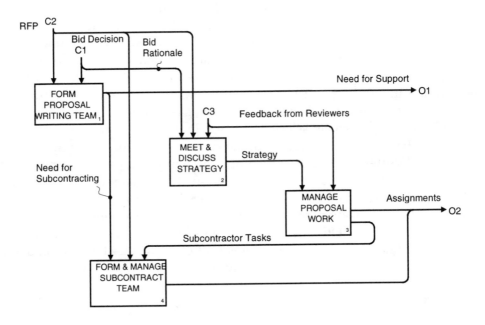

Figure 2-2: Organize & Manage the Effort.

The preponderance of problems typically occurred in the writing of individual proposal sections. Specifically, configuration management of the pieces of the proposal needed more careful attention. In this enterprise, all proposal documents were prepared using the services of a separate publications department. Often, the entire staff of the technical publications department would edit a single proposal's text and artwork; changes to the same section were sometimes submitted by more than one person; and time would be lost in reworking the edits of inexperienced temporary staff.

Instead of modeling the AS-IS chaos—an activity that would have been difficult and unproductive—we decided to develop a configuration management (CM) process based on the company's CM support tool and the know-how of the software development staff; the goal was to implement control procedures similar to those used to manage large software system source file databases. We determined that a control procedure must require check-out of proposal pieces and must restrict access until changes have been incorporated. Fortunately, the CM of software source programs had an existing IDEF0 model as a starting point (see Appendix B).

Case 3: Analyze Performance

The same enterprise had operated at a loss in a few of its field offices for several years but was unable to determine how to reverse the trend. Examination of the generic enterprise model did not provide any help in identifying where additional modeling could be used to uncover the source of the problem. Furthermore, there were no obvious technical or management problems that made one field office less profitable than another.

The problem was suspected to be caused by human factors, since it was well known that staff members at the troubled field offices had neither good working relationships with each other nor a good image with their customers. Analysts had for years thrown up their hands and declared that these factors were impossible to diagnose since they were not susceptible to logical cause-and-effect analysis.

However, the IDEF0 method allows analysts to adopt a viewpoint that controls which aspects of the model to include or exclude, and that allows them to determine which activities to emphasize. The analysts decided to model the field office operation from a human-factors viewpoint, emphasizing the activities that relate to public image, customer relations, and working relationships. Figure 2-3, titled "Develop Company's Public Image," was the result of the human-factors modeling effort.

The figure shows that six activities were selected, beginning with the staff's becoming known to the government program office through the efforts of the enterprise's marketing staff (see box 1). The technical staff supports the marketing staff when called on to speak to a selected audience at the program office. When an RFP is issued by the program office, the enterprise has its next opportunity to make an impression by pursuing the proposal submitted by the enterprise (see box 2).

If the enterprise is awarded the contract, the technical staff develops the product prescribed in the contract (see box 3), and produces the resulting Delivered Product, which then leaves an impression with staff at the government program office when they start using the product. An impression is also made during the product development effort, through the many telephone calls, draft deliverables, manager-to-manager conversations, and financial interchanges (see box 5). By the time the contract has run its course, the program office will have this experience to compare with that of working with many other contractors, and undoubtedly it will know whether the enterprise is easy to work with or not.

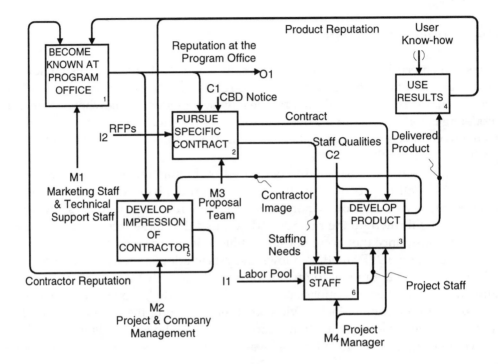

Figure 2-3: Develop Company's Public Image.

So many of the impressions made by the entire enterprise have to do with individual staff members—in the way they comport themselves, how well they communicate with each other and the program office staff, and so on—that a sixth box (HIRE STAFF) was added to the diagram. This staff-hiring function provides the project with staff, keeping details of each office's staff qualifications for reference when interviewing and selecting candidates.

To evaluate each field office, we added values for each of the data interface arrows on the diagram. The field offices that were having trouble had values such as "hard to work with" (output of box 5) and "large; slow response; not very user-friendly products" (output of box 4). The surprising result was the clear difference in "staff qualities." Those field offices that were having image problems had not focused on qualities such as "ability to work together," "ability to communicate," or "ability to make good presentations." They instead had focused too heavily on technical excellence.

As it turned out, the overemphasis on technical quality resulted in a staff that formed cliques and lacked respect for their customers' business issues and human factors. Their only interest was technical excellence, and they were not concerned if they appeared abrasive when talking to the customer.

Once the hiring-criteria problem was corrected, the enterprise's management decided that an additional IDEF0 model would be useful to ensure proper interfacing between headquarters and the field offices. This new model, again to be prepared from a human-factors viewpoint, would emphasize the activities that motivated field office managers, and would reveal what effect these motivators had on how managers run an office. In this way of thinking, guided by the model, field office managers were motivated to seek continual improvement as well as improved communication with top management at headquarters.

The model that resulted from this effort was used to plan management incentives, including objective success criteria for the operations under each manager's control. The diagrams on the following pages show the structure of the model (its node diagram), followed by the next three top levels of the model, called the motivational factor models (or "MOT," for motivation).

Figure 2-4: Node Diagram of Hiring Model.

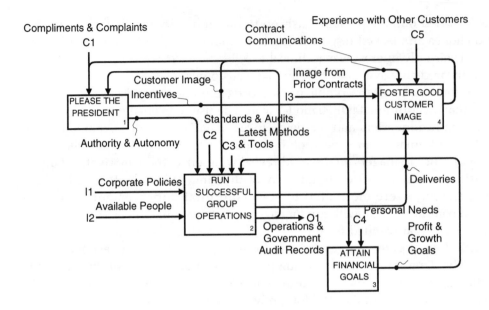

Figure 2-5: Be a Successful Group General Manager.

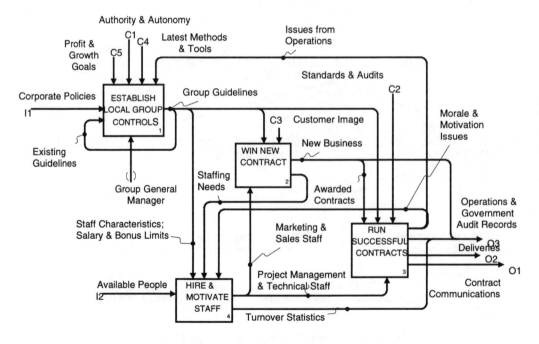

Figure 2-6: Run Successful Group Operations.

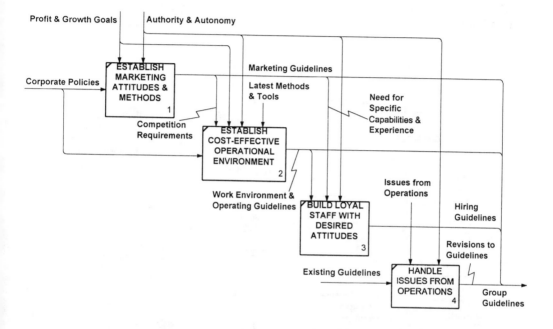

Figure 2-7: Establish Local Group Controls.

Case 4: Introduce Business Process Concepts

In order to create a Total Quality Management (TQM) program, each staff member in the enterprise was asked to think about ways that the material and information received from suppliers could be improved and about ways that the products to customers could be improved. Before this program could be implemented and operate effectively, the process needed an infrastructure, such as organizational entities with defined responsibilities and authority, channels for communicating recommendations and keeping the staff informed of progress, measurement of effectiveness of improvements, and evidence of appreciation for good suggestions from staff members. This infrastructure was modeled by showing a new environment at the top of the original model.[7] In this new environment, the continual

---

[7] The term "environment" is the SADT concept that any model fits into a bigger picture. The author determines the bounds of the model—what is included and what is outside the model's scope. The top of the model defines the model's interfaces to the world outside the scope of the model, known as its environment.

review of suggestions was shown, along with the change-planning activity, the provision for upgrading the enabling methods, and the tools required to operate in a more efficient manner (see Figure 2-8, "Evolve the Enterprise Over Time"). Figure 2-9, the final item in the set, is a TO-BE diagram detailing the five new management functions envisioned.

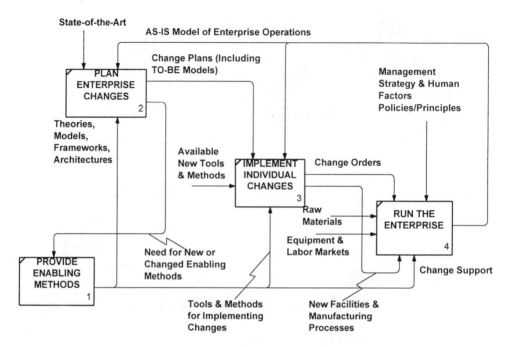

Figure 2-8: Evolve the Enterprise Over Time.

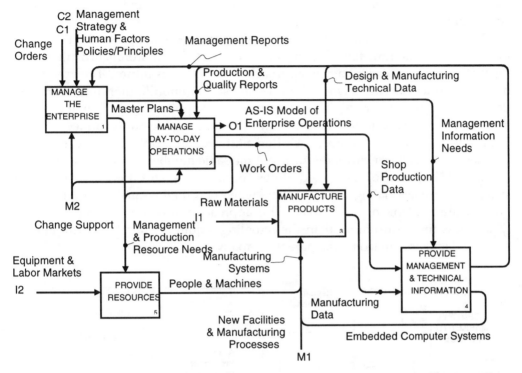

Figure 2-9: Run the Enterprise.

The enterprise next defined a new management concept to make itself more flexible, agile, and ready to respond to sudden changes in strategy from international competitors. This new picture of top enterprise management was captured in a TO-BE model showing the new flexible management structure (see Figure 2-10, "Manage the Enterprise").

Boxes 2, 3, and 4 in Figure 2-10 represent newly defined TO-BE management functions. These activities are designed to discard the concept of developing the entire product within the company and, instead, employ the more flexible approach of purchasing product parts from outside suppliers at the best possible international market price.

To control its own destiny while still producing a better product with high customer demand, the enterprise worked with the customer to define the next generation product. A decomposition of box 3 would show how this works. Once this product definition—with new customer features—has been completed, negotiations with various component suppliers are conducted (see box 4). Alternative sources of components may be sought, and small, trial production runs done until the market has been fully tested and the product durability and usability evaluated (see box 5).

The detailed decomposition of these major activities is not presented here. The idea is to illustrate how IDEF0 might be used in a TO-BE environment with a commercial enterprise to adopt a new approach to mapping its future. The example is based upon a real case: One of the Japanese automobile manufacturers has demonstrated that, by using the "large number of suppliers" approach, it can produce better-quality automobiles and can introduce new features to meet market demands more rapidly than its United States competitors. In addition, the Japanese manufacturer currently turns out the same number of cars with a fraction of the full-time staff of its United States counterparts, and it ensures a flexible structure by renegotiating with suppliers when new, higher-quality product components are available on the market. This approach is less cumbersome, less costly, and less time-consuming than the retooling required when the entire auto is fabricated and assembled by the parent company.

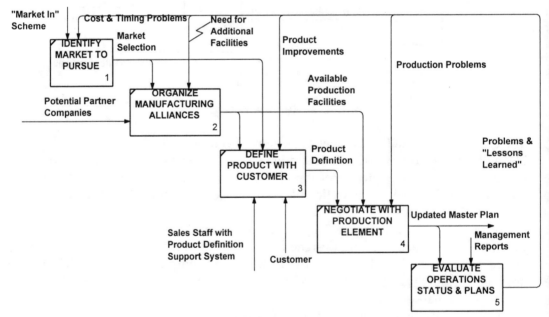

Figure 2-10: Manage the Enterprise.

Conclusions from Commercial and DoD BPR Efforts to Date

Prominent consultants in both commercial and government arenas agree that there are two main roadblocks to achieving successful BPR. First, there is the difficulty of gaining and maintaining management commitment to BPR; second, there is the difficulty of effecting the required change in the culture of an enterprise.[8] To these I would add an additional roadblock that crops up following the initial BPR analysis: the difficulty of implementing the resulting changes at minimum cost and with minimum breakage.

An interview with a top official at one of the large accounting firms confirms my contention. Our company was considering entering into an alliance with the accounting firm to implement pieces of Reengineered Enterprises (our expertise was in the areas of system integration, computer facility downsizing, and software system development). The accounting firm official would not consider our proposition since, in his words, "we have our hands full already with what we've got. Besides, our business is to develop the BPR document and then get out before taking on the hard part of implementing the results." He further went on to say that the potential for failure, cost overruns, encountering unforeseen problems, and so on, was too great a risk. His firm was happy with producing the recommendations and then getting out before they got into trouble by implementing anything.

The difficulty in implementing BPR changes was further emphasized by the president of a prominent software development assessment firm. This firm is one of the eight assessment specialist companies originally certified by the Software Engineering Institute (SEI) to perform assessments on software developers, using the government-sponsored SEI assessment procedure. After conducting assessments of more than twenty diverse software developers, the assessment firm observed that the majority of these evaluated companies did not follow through by implementing the recommended changes. The difficulty of implementing the changes soon became the assessment firm's focus, and it selected the IDEF0 methods to model implementation planning. The method was determined to be the best means of defining and obtaining buy-in on the specific changes and how they would be implemented.

---

[8] At the 1993 IDEF Users Group Conference, John Zachman made the point that change will never be implemented unless management can see that the pain resulting from *not* implementing the change exceeds the pain encountered in *making* the change.

If the human-factors roadblocks can be overcome, then the probability of successful BPR projects can be significantly increased. The IDEF0 approach, when properly applied by experienced analysts as a supporting method and expressive medium to bridge the communication gap, can accomplish great changes.[9]

---

[9] For a thorough analysis of the human factors, see Prof. John P. Kotter's article entitled "Why Transformation Efforts Fail" (*Harvard Business Review*, March/April 1995).

Features and Benefits of the IDEF0 Activity Modeling Method

CHAPTER 3

This chapter presents the basic principles of IDEF0—the assumptions behind its graphics and the rules for applying its analytical process. Expanding on Chapter 1, the discussion examines the scope of topics that can be handled by IDEF0, the benefits of its use, and a comparison to other popular graphical diagramming methods. Chapter 4 gets even more specific as it presents the detailed syntax and semantics of the IDEF0 graphical language, as officially defined in the Federal Standard.

The Seven Basic Principles

There are seven principles—or rules of conduct—that must be followed in order to apply IDEF0 techniques successfully:

1. *The method must accurately represent the problem area:* A graphical model of a system should be developed so that the system elements and their interactions can be defined, documented, communicated, discussed, and analyzed effectively.
2. *The model must have a top-down, modular, hierarchical structure*: The model should depict the system top-down by defining modular system elements that interact to form a hierarchy.
3. *The model must separate function from design:* By definition, *what* the system does (function) must be kept separate from *how* it does it

(design). That is, more than one design can be developed for a single function; this distinction is important. Because of this, design improvements may be developed without disturbing the basic function. If a more drastic (functional) change is called for, then basic functions can be changed and a new design created to meet the new functional requirements.

4. *The model must reflect both objects and actions—things and happenings*: The modeling method must be able to depict all forms of things and happenings. Restriction of the modeling scope to raw data would leave out the people, resources, raw materials, human factors, and other important influences on the operation of the enterprise, all of which are critical in managing change.

5. *The model form must be graphical:* The form on which the model is recorded must be graphical, not mathematical or textual. The graphical form must communicate concisely and rigorously to the people who must validate that the model reflects the real functions and processes of the enterprise.

6. *The model must be the product of disciplined, coordinated teamwork:* To build a model and to achieve consensus among the enterprise staff requires disciplined, coordinated teamwork. The IDEF0 method must therefore contain the working rules and procedures for developing and validating the model in an organized way (reader/author cycle forms and procedures, librarian configuration management procedures, and the like).

7. *The model must present all information in writing:* By having a standardized form on which all information (interview notes, conclusions with their rationale, definitions of terms, and so on) is retained, the method assures that information is not lost during the early stages of the planning cycle. With its forms and procedures, IDEF0 provides a convenient means of retaining information.

Scope of Subject Matter That Can Be Handled by IDEF0

As we have stated, IDEF0 is a method for analyzing enterprises. An enterprise may be a company, a division of a company, a group of companies working together in a joint venture, a field office of a parent company, a support function within an office (for example, publications, accounting, or payroll), a government agency (for example, the Department of Defense or the Commerce Department), an individual running a small business, or a project within a company. All of these are enterprises, since they are composed of one or more people working to accomplish some form of product development or to provide some service.

The scope of the analysis encompasses manual as well as computerized aspects of the enterprise. IDEF0 is particularly useful for rigorously defining the juncture at which manual actions interface with the computer (the so-called man-machine interface). For example, using the *viewpoint* concept of IDEF0, the author may develop a model from the user's viewpoint as well as from the software developer's viewpoint, thus providing a requirements definition from both important aspects of a software system to be developed. The model bridges the communication gap between user and software cultures.

IDEF0 analysis does not stop at the man-machine interface, but may be used to model the operation of the software system itself. In fact, the method has been successfully used for many years to model the requirements, top-level design, and detailed design of software systems.

Benefits Resulting from the Use of IDEF0

The primary goal of IDEF0 is to facilitate change management, a goal that was introduced in Chapter 2, under the topic "Use of IDEF0 for Military Downsizing and Reorganization." In this chapter, we discuss specific benefits that can be expected from the IDEF0 modeling effort.

Stated simply, the goal of the modeling effort must not stop at developing a model. Such a goal leads to models that sit on a shelf and do not achieve real operational benefits. Instead, the purpose of an IDEF0 model should be "to provide a baseline on which to plan and manage change." The model serves as a communication vehicle for streamlining existing processes, for introducing new technology, for evaluating the impact of a change on related processes, and for achieving consensus among the staff involved in the change.

The initial benefits are achieved by the analyst as he creates (authors) the model. In developing the model, the analyst cannot help but identify problems and potential improvements in the operation of the enterprise. When the analysis is complete, the paper model is available, thereby providing documentation on-the-fly and not requiring a separate, after-the-fact documentation phase at the end of the analysis. Specific benefits of IDEF0 modeling are as follows:

> *Identifies Needs:* A good IDEF0 model will look very simple and easy to understand. Needs and opportunities for improvement revealed during the modeling effort may seem obvious at first, but they would have gone unnoticed otherwise.

Builds Consensus: The diversity of a staff's background, training, skills, and knowledge can impair communication.   The reader/author model critique method can establish a well-defined common basis for understanding by the entire staff. Real consensus, not just imagined consensus, can be reached.

Enhances Vision: The condensed, graphical picture provided by the model presents a thought-provoking baseline on which to consider improvements. An analyst or an enterprise planner who considers potential use of a new technology or new method in light of this baseline may identify specific application opportunities.

Provides a Basis for an Open Architecture: The model structure may be used to define the interfaces between system elements, and to identify precise interfaces for the definition of an open systems architecture. The model bounds the scope precisely by showing where the modeled system fits into the bigger picture.

Broadens Automation and Commonality Potential: Almost any model of any size will reveal activities that are similar to those already modeled in other parts of the structure. These similarities can be used to define improvements, such as a subsystem to support these common activities.

Supports Management Control Through Metrics: The model may serve as a baseline for cost, time, flow capacity, peak loads, and other metrics relevant to the design of a new system. If the model detail is not sufficient to attach specific metrics, the lack of detail should be used to identify where further decomposition is needed. Finer detail in the modeling will facilitate more precise measurement.

Defines Variants for Broader Support System Use: Support systems that are applied to several activities in the model may benefit from a careful analysis of the actual functionality needed at each point of usage. Variants and versions of the support system could save considerable cost if the support system can be fine-tuned for each specific usage point.

Features of IDEF0 Analysis

The IDEF0 method analyzes a subject by investigating how it operates, by modeling the operational details uncovered, and by applying evaluation techniques (such as "value added" criteria) to identify potential improvements. The author of the model uses two-dimensional, simple graphics as a means of capturing and communicating the results of the analysis.

Applying IDEF0 to the analysis of an enterprise thus results in a paper, two-dimensional graphical model of the enterprise. The model is hierarchical in nature, consisting of a set of diagrams in which each diagram represents three to six activities of the enterprise. At the top of the IDEF0 model, the enterprise is decomposed into three to six very large activities or subsystems that represent the activities of the enterprise (see Figure 3-1). These activities are shown as rectangular boxes.

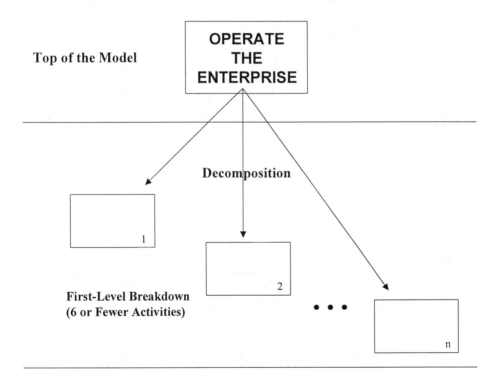

Figure 3-1: Breakdown into Six or Fewer Activities.

Once the top-level activity breakdown has reached consensus among the enterprise staff, each of the boxes is further broken down into the next level of detail on a new three-to-six activity diagram. Thus, the entire IDEF0 model provides a tree structure of diagrams. Anyone wishing to inspect a particular aspect of the enterprise may scan the tree structure, identify the activity and level of detail that is useful for his purposes, and then retrieve the corresponding IDEF0 diagram to study the complete description of the selected activity at the selected level of detail. Figure 3-2 shows a graphical representation of an IDEF0 model that breaks down an enterprise into three levels of detail.

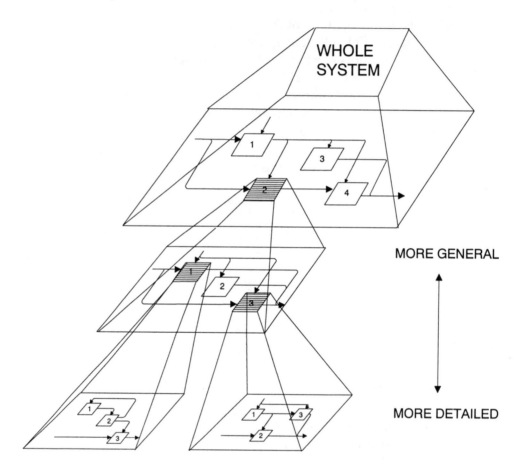

Figure 3-2: Top-Down IDEF0 Model Structure.

At the top level, the entire system being modeled (labeled Whole System in the figure) is shown as broken down into four parts, labeled 1, 2, 3, and 4. Part 2 is further broken down into a three-part diagram, shown below the initial diagram as emanating from a shaded box 2. Finally, boxes 1 and 3 of the detailed part 2 box are broken down into yet finer detail in the two diagrams displayed at the bottom of the figure. This illustrates an important feature of the IDEF0 model: Any aspect may be broken down to be as detailed as necessary, while other aspects may be less completely decomposed. This permits the analyst to zero in on the most critical aspects to be analyzed, while putting off the other aspects until needed.

Comparison to Data Flow Diagramming

Most popular in past decades, the data flow diagram approach to modeling a computer software system is still used today for software design. It provides a picture of the data that are input to and output from the software. Figure 3-3 shows that Location of Assembly and Quality Measurements are input to a Scheduling Database of information about the status of a part. When a process has been completed, the assembly machine sends a "Process Complete" Status signal to the database, as an additional input. Thus, the database has a running record of where the part is located and which processes have been performed. As output, the software produces a report on the status of the part.

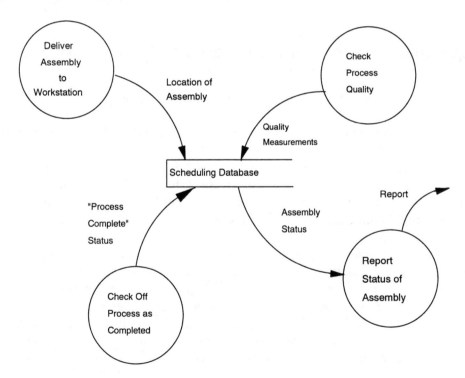

Figure 3-3: A Data Flow Diagram to Track Assembly Status.

Figure 3-4 shows the same information as Figure 3-3, but this time as an IDEF0 diagram.

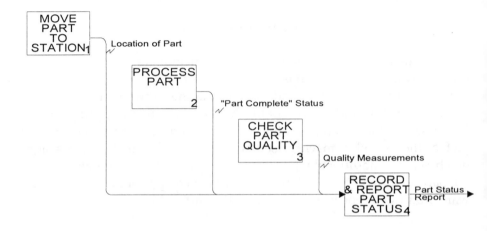

Equivalent Information to the Data Flow Diagram

Figure 3-4: Same Track Assembly Status Data Flow Using IDEF0 Format.

Note that the interfaces between the activity boxes in the IDEF0 diagram are represented by arrows, depicting one activity supplying input to or controlling one or more other activities (as we shall see in Figures 3-5 through 3-7). Unlike the simpler data flow diagram, the interactivity relationship can include data flow, raw material flow, management and other forms of control, resources (such as people, machines, and computers), and whatever else must be included to model the complete enterprise's operational details.

Figures 3-5 through 3-7 detail information that is not shown on the data flow diagram. Whereas a data flow diagram is adequate to depict information needed by a computer software program, it is not adequate for reengineering purposes, since there are other factors influencing an enterprise's operations. These other factors must be included if the reengineering process is to be understood and designed, and the changeover process controlled. The IDEF0 model shows what controls each activity and who performs it, as well as the resources needed by each activity.

Figure 3-5 shows the addition of the physical part proceeding through the stages of manufacturing, from Unassembled Part entering box 1 to Completed Part leaving box 3.

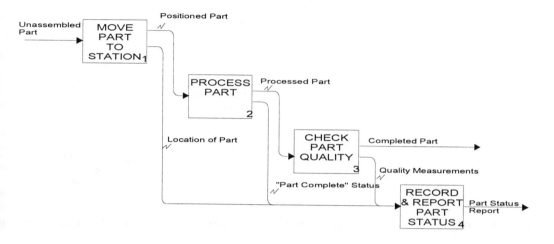

Addition of the Physical Product Being Processed

Figure 3-5: Assembly Status Tracking IDEF0
Diagram, with Physical Parts Assembly Added.

Figure 3-6 adds controls to each IDEF0 activity box. For example, we see that there is an Assembly Schedule that controls when the part is prepared for processing. Company Manuals are used to control the remaining three activities. These controls must be carefully considered when making changes, and therefore are important to include in the reengineering effort.

Finally, Figure 3-7 shows what mechanism performs each process. This includes people (for example, Test Engineers for box 3) as well as support tools and systems (for example, Testing Facilities for box 3). A common practice is to document the elements of the enterprise's organization chart as mechanisms in the model in order to show the assignment of responsibility to specific organizational elements. In the TO-BE picture, the revised organizational responsibility is likewise shown.

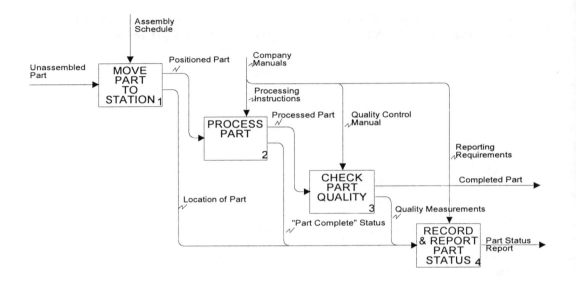

Addition of Control Information -- What Controls Each Activit

Figure 3-6: Previous Diagram, with Controls Added.

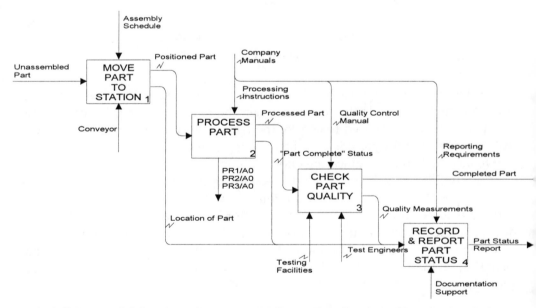

Addition of Mechanisms -- What Performs Each Activity

Figure 3-7: Complete IDEF0 Diagram, with Mechanisms Added.

An important difference between data flow diagrams and IDEF0 diagrams is the scope of the topic covered: DFDs were intended to depict fine detail needed by a software design specification, whereas IDEF0 diagrams were designed to capture very complex topics such as the operation of the aerospace industry, a government agency, or a business.

IDEF0 syntax may be used to capture fine detail, as we have just shown in the series of diagrams comparing the information content of DFDs to IDEF0 diagrams. However, many of the features of IDEF0 have the objective of handling great complexity, not depicting fine detail. The purpose and viewpoint statements of an IDEF0 model are examples of features that enable handling complexity.

While the purpose of a set of data flow diagrams is to depict the operation of computer software, the purpose of an IDEF0 model may be one of many, since the modeling method is applicable to any "system" comprised of "things" and "happenings." Focusing the analysis effort by purpose shortens the list of enterprise elements that must be modeled during a reengineering effort. In other words, the analyst must narrow the topic to be modeled and decrease complexity.

An IDEF0 model must also select a specific *viewpoint*. If all viewpoints of an enterprise were to be included in a single model, the information would be too complex to understand.

Understanding a Top-Level IDEF0 Diagram of an Enterprise

Figure 3-8 presents a typical top-level diagram in an IDEF0 model (it originally appeared as Figure 2-9). This diagram might represent the most general level of detail of a model entitled "Run the Enterprise."

The figure shows the running of an enterprise, broken down into five major functions: 1) Manage the Enterprise; 2) Manage Day-to-Day Operations; 3) Manufacture Products; 4) Provide Management & Technical Information; and 5) Provide Resources. Four of these major functions are shown as boxes positioned in a stairstep fashion that makes the control and feedback loops between the functions simpler to draw. The fifth box (Provide Resources) is shown below the stairstep, since it is a support function that provides resources (people and machines) to be used by the other functions.

By reading the names in the boxes, anyone can get a quick idea of the breakdown of the subject Run the Enterprise, as well as the topics to be modeled in subsequent lower-level diagrams. For example, if the reader wishes to examine further detail regarding the provisioning of resources, he would isolate the diagram for box 5 and study that at a finer level of detail.

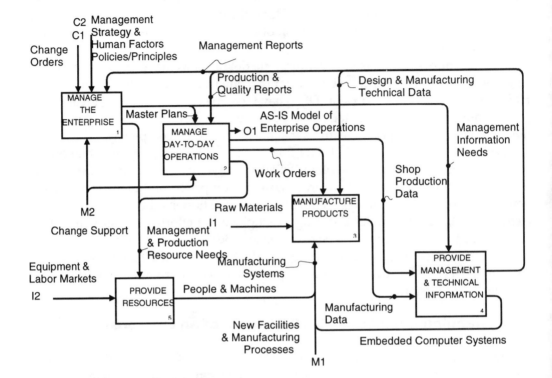

Figure 3-8: A Typical IDEF0 Diagram.

IDEF0 graphics are undeniably straightforward and that quality is, in my view, one key to their success. Such elaborations as additional box shapes, dotted arrows, and formalisms for arrow branching structures have been experimented with by modelers since the inception of IDEF0. It seems only natural to conclude that such elaborations would provide additional expressive capabilities to the analyst.

However, I have learned to resist the temptation to elaborate the syntax, since this makes the graphics too complex to fulfill the essential role of the model to communicate. At the early stages of project planning, communication is the key element, and the simple graphics that are quickly learned and employed must remain a basic element of IDEF0.

Levels of Abstraction in IDEF0 Models

As stated, the breakdown approach used in IDEF0 modeling decomposes selected activities into finer and finer levels of detail. The resultant model set includes sufficient detail to plan and control the implementation of changes to the enterprise.

An IDEF0 model may also contain multiple levels of abstraction. To understand what is meant by "level of abstraction," let's consider a typical enterprise. Each level of management has its natural level of abstraction. Top management must think in broad terms, taking into account many viewpoints as well as abstractions of the details of what is going on in the enterprise. An upper-level manager cannot possibly understand every detail of all of the activities in the entire enterprise, but he must abstract business processes and characteristics that are important at his level of abstraction. He must consider such things as overall profit, hiring policies, or the quality of the enterprise's product line, rather than the specific factors that go into these high-level abstractions.

Conversely, a manager at a lower level needs fine-level detail about a specific topic from a single viewpoint, and he may get uneasy thinking in general terms. His level of abstraction is concerned with such things as the cost of raw materials, the capabilities of specific staff members, or the quality of the service for which he is responsible.

The model's level of abstraction is independent of its level of detail. That is, after selecting a level of abstraction to model, the author may decompose the activities to whatever level of detail he requires to satisfy the purpose of the model. However, if the purpose of the model requires information at a different level of abstraction, no amount of further detailing at the present level of abstraction will provide the needed information. Modeling at all required levels of abstraction must be completed to satisfy the enterprise analysis requirements.

The IDEF0 concept of a mechanism is different from the concept of level of abstraction. In IDEF0, a mechanism represents who performs the activity and what tools (software packages and equipment) are required to perform the activity. In other words, the mechanism identifies the resources needed to perform the function. A mechanism is therefore at a lower level of abstraction than the activity box it implements.

The fact that the mechanism depicts a lower level of abstraction does not mean that it cannot be modeled in IDEF0. It just means that the mechanism is shown as an arrow entering the bottom of the box, and that a separate model must be examined to understand how the mechanism works (see Figure 3-9).

The IDEF0 diagram in Figure 3-9 shows Activity A23 (Edit Document) using the word processor support mechanism. The IDEF0 model for the word processor is shown at the lower-right corner of Figure 3-9. What this tells us is that any word processor mechanism may be modeled and plugged into the diagram to show the precise activity performed when editing a document with any variety of word processors. This shows *how* the editing is done using the mechanism, and therefore indicates that there is a drop in level of mechanization from *what* is done to the document by the EDIT activity.

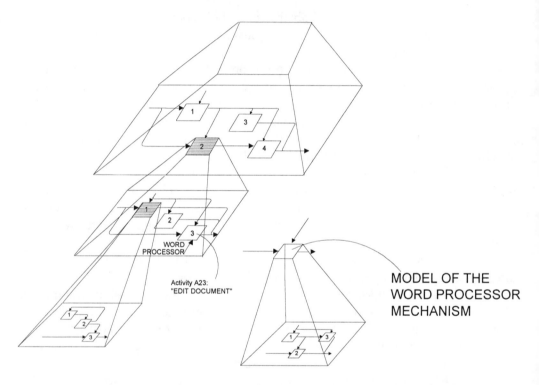

WORD
PROCESSOR

Activity A23:
"EDIT DOCUMENT"

MODEL OF THE
WORD PROCESSOR
MECHANISM

Figure 3-9: Mechanism at a Lower Level of Abstraction.

To accomplish the reengineering of an enterprise, an analyst may need to show multiple levels of abstraction and several levels of mechanism, as well as how those are integrated to perform the processes of the enterprise. Showing all this provides a clear, accurate *big picture* of the overall operation of the enterprise.

In addition to an IDEF0 process-oriented analysis, various additional analysis methods may be applied, using the IDEF0 model as a baseline. For example, the analyst may need to know where costs and labor are being expended, in order to estimate the return on investment of potential changes or to understand the impact of introducing new technology. Various analyses, such as activity-based costing (ABC) and work flow simulation, are typically applied using the IDEF0 model as a baseline.

The Role of Data Analysis Compared to IDEF0 Function Analysis

Detail needed regarding the processes requires not only IDEF0 process models, but also precise information about the arrow content. This requires a careful analysis of data.

An analyst may be confronted with a tidal wave of raw data when he first gathers information about an enterprise. He typically starts by finding out the precise meaning of the terms that are key to the system's operation; then he documents these definitions. Once he has done that, he has a solid basis for initiating discussion with the staff about the detailed operation of the system. But even before analyzing the system in detail, he must consider the system functions and their interactions to understand the need, the purpose, and the objective of the relevant data.

Not all analysts take this view. In fact, some prominent leaders in the database community have stated that there is no need to look at the functions and activities at all. One database proponent wrote that the development of a function model actually gets in the way of the programmer and should be avoided if possible, further proclaiming his First Rule of CASE: "Only one diagramming method is needed—the data model—and code can be generated automatically from a data model."[1]

This statement is true if the automated system to be built performs simple, well-known processes such as basic banking transactions (for example, put money in checking account, withdraw money from checking account, transfer money to savings account, and so on). These activities are so familiar that an IDEF0 model would not be helpful, and design of the data structure of the system can be started almost immediately. The statement is not true, however, if the software to be built has a complex processing aspect, such as that for an avionics system or a computer's operating system.

The field of automated programming would also lead one to believe that analysis, design, and programming are outmoded—as if the system will do all this for you and produce a running computer program. However, the type of system that is implied here is one that simply queries a database and displays answers on a screen. Automatic programming has a long way to go before it can build an avionics system, a computer operating system, or a compiler. And haven't we slipped into the solution domain? Automated programming tools are of no help if you are trying to reengineer a business operation and have not yet understood what the system will look like.

---

[1] Clive Finkelstein, *An Introduction to Information Engineering: From Strategic Planning to Information Systems* (Reading, Mass.: Addison-Wesley, 1989), p. 376.

Regardless of the system to be analyzed and the comparative importance of the data versus the activity analysis, at some point the data must be analyzed. To perform this portion of the analysis, the analyst must understand several important characteristics of the data.

Although there are many data characteristics that could be analyzed, two are critical: data dynamics and data structure. Data dynamics can be depicted by SADT data models, using a portion of SADT that was not adopted by the Air Force for IDEF0. Data structure may be modeled using IDEF1X, where the term "structure" signifies all non-dynamic data information, such as its attributes and its relationship to other data elements.

A type of function model, the SADT data model shows the breakdown of the kinds of data in the system, with arrows indicating which activities produce which data elements and which activities use the data for what purpose. This gives a dynamic picture of the data being created, used, and merged with other data to form new data entities. The SADT data model is a natural companion for an IDEF0 or SADT activity model, and it is useful for analyzing how the system manipulates data and what is affected when changes are implemented. It also provides a validation of the activity model. In fact, most data models developed using SADT result in corrections to the activity model!

The IDEF1X model provides all of the structural information about the data. Ultimately, relating the need for and the usage of specific attributes of data by the activity boxes of an IDEF0 model is the key to integrating the two models.

IDEF0 Graphic Language Syntax and Semantics

CHAPTER 4

The syntax and semantics for both IDEF0 diagrams and IDEF0 models are precisely defined in the FIPS for IDEF0.[1] The summary presented in this chapter is intended to provide sufficient practical detail for the IDEF0 modeler, but modelers should refer to the FIPS itself for a more complete definition.

As we have seen in previous chapters, IDEF0 models are made up of diagrams arranged in a hierarchical structure. IDEF0 diagrams are made up of boxes and arrows, where the boxes represent the happenings (activities) and the arrows represent the interfaces between those happenings—the things. Each diagram tells a story about a portion of the system being modeled. The top-most diagram represents the entire system, and each box on this top diagram is decomposed into subordinate models at the next finer level of detail. This succession of decompositions forms the hierarchical model structure.

Each IDEF0 diagram is presented on a sheet of paper called a diagram form. In the following section of this chapter, the elements of an individual IDEF0 diagram (the box and the arrow) are defined. In succeeding sections, these elements are used to create diagrams, and the diagrams are then structured to form a complete IDEF0 model.

---

[1] *FIPS PUB 183: Integration Definition for Function Modeling (IDEF0)*, U.S. Department of Commerce, Technology Administration, National Institute of Standards and Technology (Washington, D.C.: 1993).

Activity Box Syntax

Rules applying to the elements of an activity box syntax are given below and are shown in the generically labeled Figure 4-1.

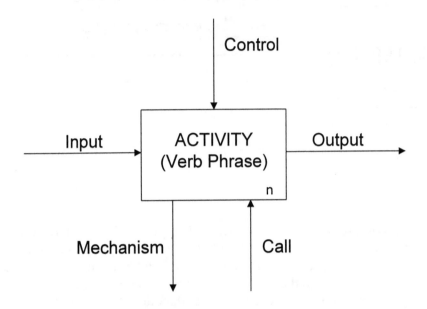

Figure 4-1: Activity Box Syntax.

1. A box is named by an active verb or verb phrase.
2. A box has a number (1 to 6), which appears in its lower-right corner.
3. Input is converted by the activity to produce the output, under the direction of the control information.
4. Each of the four sides of the box may have one or more arrows, with the following meaning:

     •   Arrows entering the left side of the box indicate input.
     •   Arrows leaving the right side of the box represent output.
     •   Arrows entering the top of the box show control.
     •   Arrows entering the bottom of the box indicate mechanism, that is, the *what* and *how* of enterprise activity.
     •   Arrows leaving the bottom of the box are call arrows, which indicate where to look for further detail about the activity.

5. Each arrow segment may be labeled with a noun or noun phrase that describes the contents of the arrow.

In SADT, the space outside and below the lower-right corner of the box is used to show where further detail may be found about the activity represented by the box. This convention was not adopted in the IDEF0 standard, but I do use it throughout this book to show that a decomposition exists, or to indicate where to look elsewhere for more detail (a document, military standard, or other model, for example). In practice, however, the convention changes depending on which software modeling tool is being used to develop the IDEF0 model.

The SADT convention for showing that an activity is decomposed is to write a number just below the right side of the box. This number is the C-number, the sequential identifier of the diagram that appears in the lower-right corner of the diagram form. We will see later in this book how this location is used to indicate other forms of links to other models or documents that provide further detail about the activity.

Arrow Syntax Elements

The following rules apply to arrow syntax.

1. Arrows are drawn horizontally or vertically.
2. Curved arrows have corners rounded at a 90 degree arc.
3. Each arrow must have a label describing its content, and this label must be unique throughout the entire model.
4. Arrows that attach to a box at both ends on a single diagram are called internal arrows.
5. Arrows having one end unattached to any box on a single diagram are called boundary arrows, since they represent things entering or leaving the context of that diagram.
6. Arrows having one end unattached at the top-most diagram (called the A-0 diagram) are external arrows, since they represent things entering or leaving the context of the whole model.

Figure 4-2 illustrates the shapes of these arrows.

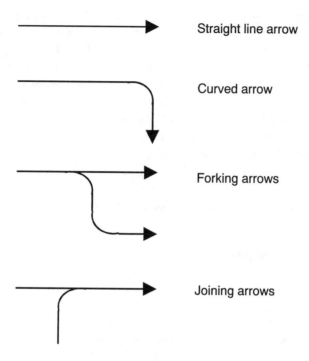

Figure 4-2: Arrow Syntax.

Figure 4-3 shows that arrows can be conduits for other arrows, which may, in turn, contain other arrows. At the top levels of an IDEF0 model, these conduits are large bundles of arrows that match the level of abstraction of the high-level activity boxes. As the model is decomposed, forking arrows break out of the larger conduit and feed to the appropriate activity boxes. Likewise, the precise arrow content produced by an activity box, shown leaving the box, bundles with other arrows to form a new conduit.

Arrows that fork from a conduit or join into multiple branches indicate that all data contained in the main branch may flow through all branches. If not all of the content flows through, a restrictive label must be added on the subsidiary branch. Figure 4-3 gives an example: The name Writing Instruments appears on the main branch of the arrow (see the upper right illustration in Figure 4-3), but the Pencils label, written on the branch, shows that only pencils flow in the branch.

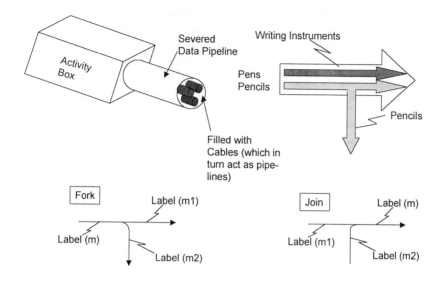

Figure 4-3: Semantics of Arrow Forks and Joins.

We now have defined the basic elements of an IDEF0 diagram—boxes and arrows. To form a diagram, we lay out three to six activity boxes in a stairstep fashion on a diagram form, and then add the arrows representing the interfaces between the boxes. Together, these depict the complete story told by the diagram.

The three-six rule ("No diagram shall have fewer than three or more than six boxes") has great significance in fulfilling the communication power requirement for IDEF0. That is, if fewer than three activities are included in a breakdown, it provides too little new information to be worthwhile; if more than six activities are in the breakdown, then the story is too complex to be conveyed well. The three-six rule has another significant benefit: It results in diagrams that can be copied on a standard 8 ½" x 11" sheet of paper. Since one of the basic procedures of IDEF0 is the reader/author critique, this ability to copy and distribute models is critical to the method's practicality.

The IDEF0 Diagram Form

Figure 4-4 shows the IDEF0 diagram form. Divided into three full-width horizontal sections, the form consists of a temporary working information region (top), a message region (center), and an identification region (bottom). The boxes and arrows are drawn in the message region; the diagram's position in the model hierarchy is recorded in the identification region, and the temporary working information (such as, project and author names, creation date, level of approval, and revision history) is recorded in the top region. Once the model is ready for publication, this top region, containing temporary information, can be removed, since it is no longer of interest.

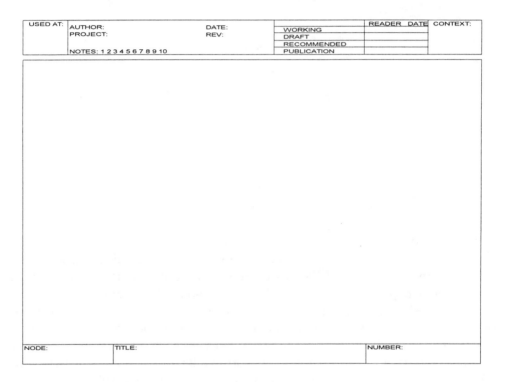

Figure 4-4: The IDEF0 Diagram Form.

The identification region is further divided into three parts containing three types of information: the node number, which gives the position of the diagram in the model structure; the name of the diagram, which must be identical to the box that is being decomposed on the parent diagram; and the diagram number, which identifies the specific sheet of paper. If several different versions of a diagram are created, each will have the same node number and the same name, but each will carry a unique identification number in the lower right-hand corner of the diagram.

The diagram number is typically composed of either the author's C-number (his initials, followed by the next number of a numerical sequence) or the page number on which the diagram is printed in the final distributed document. The C-number is used while the model is being developed and is assigned by the author each time he starts a new diagram for any purpose. This convention is important for record-keeping purposes and to assure proper configuration management over the model master copy.

The C-number may be figured manually or it may be automatically increased to the next number in the author's diagram log. Originally, the diagram log was a paper log, but in most cases now, the log is automated through the use of software modeling tools that automatically assign a new number each time the author calls for a blank diagram. The C-number convention originated in SADT, but it was not adopted when the Air Force initiated IDEF0.

The author uses the message region in the center of a second copy of the form to write text about the diagram. When the diagram is finished and published, the text form accompanies the diagram on a facing page, so the reader can study the diagram and text simultaneously, without flipping pages.

The diagram text is not written until the diagram itself has become stable. This occurs late in the reader/author review cycle, when the system experts have validated the diagram, and when the diagram is no longer likely to be changed significantly.

The purpose of the diagram text is to highlight features of the diagram and to facilitate correct presentation of the facts, but all information must be contained on the diagram itself. The text is not intended to expand on the information given in the diagram, nor should it describe what each activity box on the diagram represents—this latter job belongs to the decomposition diagram, as we will see below.

Figure 4-5 depicts the process of authoring IDEF0 models and is used here to illustrate the general structure of a diagram in final publication format. The diagram in Figure 4-5 contains five boxes (conforming to the three-six rule), with a verb phrase inside each box describing one activity. These five sub-activities make up the single activity PRACTICE IDEF0. The diagram displays a typical structure of branching and joining arrows, showing interfaces between activities. As was noted earlier in this chapter, arrows that are connected to boxes at both ends are internal to the diagram; arrows with one unconnected end are boundary arrows, whether or not they are coming from or going to the external environment of the diagram.

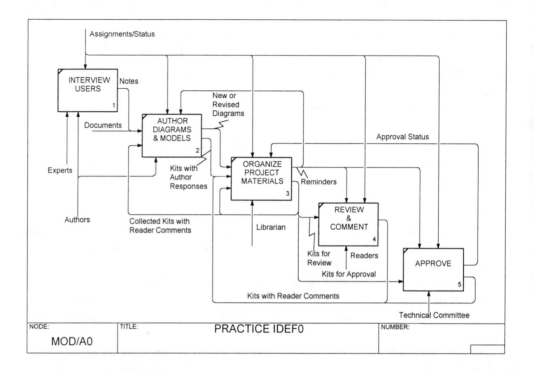

Figure 4-5: Diagram of the IDEF0 Modeling Process.

In Figure 4-5, control arrows entering the tops of boxes show assignments, reminders from the librarian, and approval status. An arrow join is shown near the left side of box 2, where documents and notes join to provide the primary input to the authoring process. A fork is shown in the same area, where the arrow mechanism labeled Authors forks and is shown performing both interviewing (box 1) and authoring (box 2) activities. As you read this chapter, continue to study the diagram for a preliminary view of the process of operating an IDEF0 project. We will return to this figure later, after we've completed the description of the modeling process.

Earlier in this chapter, we saw how the text form and the diagram represent the same information in the published model. Copies of the same form may also be used to record two additional kinds of information: glossary entries and for-exposition-only (FEO) diagrams.

The glossary that accompanies a diagram defines the box names and arrow labels used on that diagram. Once a model is finished and ready for publication, glossaries for individual diagrams are merged into a single, large glossary for the entire model. An FEO diagram can be attached to a diagram to emphasize some particular fact that furthers the purpose of the model. A typical FEO might contain a copy of the diagram with the main path of arrows highlighted, a particular subset of the diagram describing a critical event, or a raveled-rope picture of the contents of an arrow conduit showing all the individual arrows conveyed by a large pipeline.

IDEF0 Model Rules

Now that we have defined the full set of IDEF0 diagram rules, let us look next at the rules for IDEF0 models. We know that IDEF0 models are comprised of diagrams that are integrated into a top-down, hierarchical structure, as shown in Figure 4-6 (seen earlier at Figure 3-2).

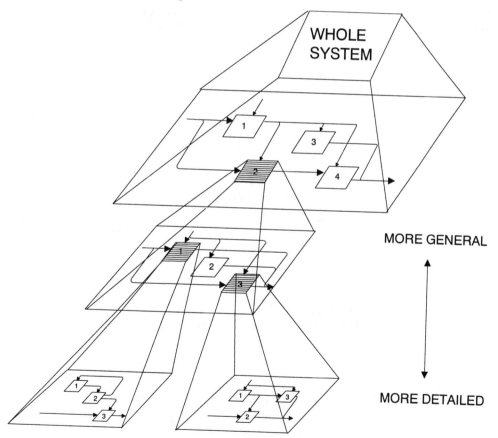

Figure 4-6: Model Structure of Diagrams.

Each diagram represents the breakdown, or decomposition, of a box in the next higher, or parent, diagram level. If a reader wishes to explore details of any element of the system, he may select a diagram, a box on that diagram, the decomposition of the box, a box on that decomposed diagram, and so on, until he reaches the needed level of detail.

The top-most box in a model has box number 0. It appears on a diagram form all by itself and represents the entire system. The diagram for this box has the node number A-0 (pronounced "A minus zero"), where the A signifies an activity model, and the "minus sign zero" signifies the top of the model. The purpose and viewpoint of the model are also recorded as textual annotations on this top-most diagram, since they apply to the entire model. (See Figure 4-7.)

The structure of a model is defined and referenced by node numbers. Each box in the model is a node in the model structure and has a unique node number. If a diagram is decomposed to reveal greater detail, then that new diagram has the same node number as its parent box. To determine the new box's node number, simply append the box number (which is between one and six) to the diagram's node number.

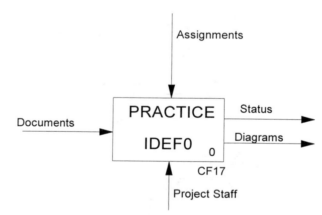

Purpose: This model will be used to train staff
            in the Operation of an IDEF0 Project

Viewpoint: The Project Manager

Figure 4-7: A-0 Diagram with Purpose and Viewpoint.

The decomposition diagram that shows the first-level breakdown of the top box is called A0 (pronounced "A zero"). Each of the up to six boxes on this diagram is then numbered 1 up to 6, from upper left to lower right. The decomposition diagram of each of these boxes is thus numbered A1, A2, on up to A6.

Figure 4-8 shows this structure graphically in the form of a node diagram. The node diagram is often used as a table of contents for an IDEF0 model. It is very useful for scanning the breadth and depth of the entire model and then for selecting specific diagrams to examine more closely.

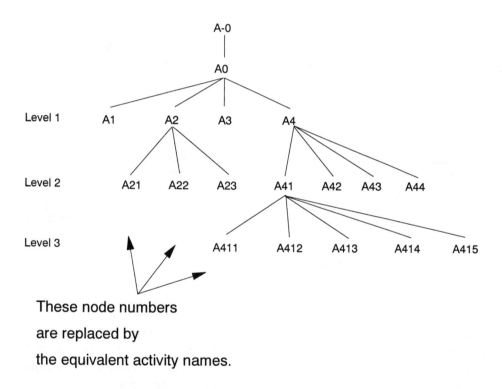

Figure 4-8: Node Structure of a Model.

Figure 4-8 shows the pattern of node numbers at each level of detail of a model. If this were an actual node diagram, the name of the box would appear instead of the node number, since the activity name is the item of interest. Figure 4-9 (seen earlier as Figure 2-4) shows how names would be substituted to create an actual node diagram. (Node diagrams are discussed more fully in Chapter 5.)

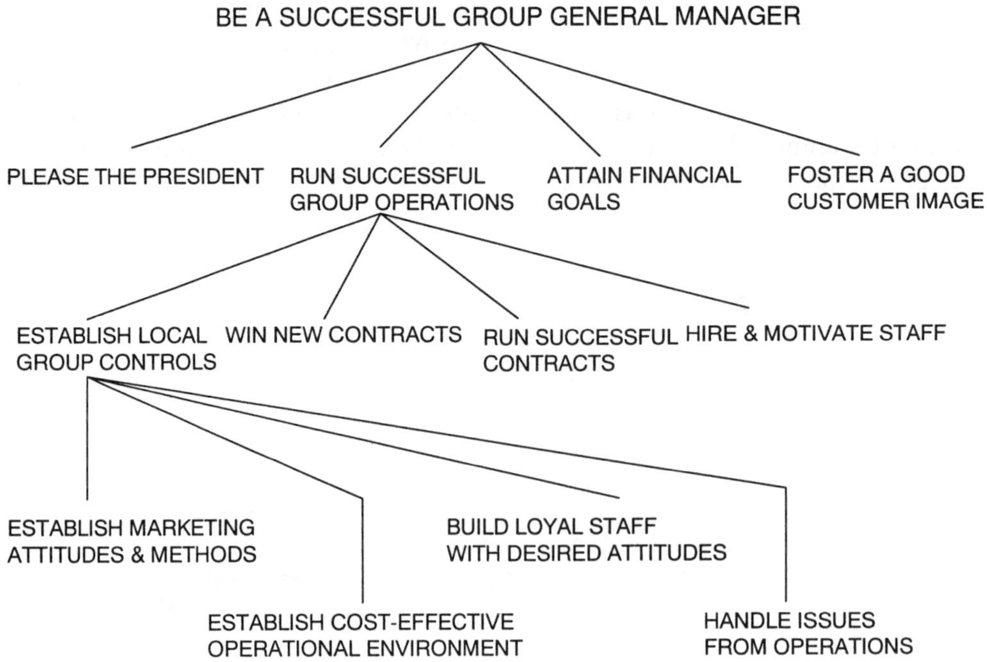

BE A SUCCESSFUL GROUP GENERAL MANAGER

PLEASE THE PRESIDENT   RUN SUCCESSFUL   ATTAIN FINANCIAL   FOSTER A GOOD
                         GROUP OPERATIONS   GOALS   CUSTOMER IMAGE

ESTABLISH LOCAL   WIN NEW CONTRACTS   RUN SUCCESSFUL HIRE & MOTIVATE STAFF
GROUP CONTROLS   CONTRACTS

ESTABLISH MARKETING   BUILD LOYAL STAFF
ATTITUDES & METHODS   WITH DESIRED ATTITUDES

        ESTABLISH COST-EFFECTIVE   HANDLE ISSUES
        OPERATIONAL ENVIRONMENT   FROM OPERATIONS

Figure 4-9: Sample Node Diagram.

We have stated that a node number identifies a specific box or diagram in the model. However, a more complete reference language is needed to enable an author who is writing, say, glossary definitions or intermodel references to refer to a specific box, arrow, or arrow segment. This language, called the "model reference language," permits the author to identify specific input, control, output, or mechanism arrows by means of a code, as follows: Numbering clockwise around the outside of a box and assigning a letter according to the referenced side (I for input, C for control, O for output, and M for mechanism, or ICOM for short), the author defines the referenced side of the box. The arrow head or tail is then further identified by numbering left-to-right and top-to-bottom. This results in a two-character identifier of the form "letter digit" (for example I1, C2, or M1), which totally describes the arrow's position relative to the box, without requiring the author to write anything more on the diagram. Figure 4-10 illustrates the approach.

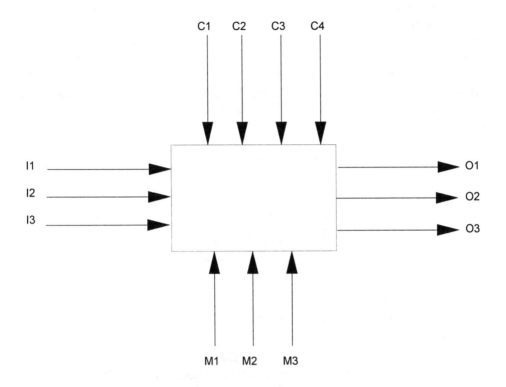

Figure 4-10: ICOM Code Definition.

By combining the node-numbering language for identifying a box or diagram with ICOM-coding language for identifying a specific arrow head or tail, we now have a very concise textual language for defining any precise spot in an IDEF0 model.

The most common use of this reference language is in a *detailed reference expression* (DRE) to refer to remote diagram locations in a model.

Because IDEF0 was created as a high-level method for modeling and analyzing complex systems, it does not contain specific syntax and semantics for particular forms of design solutions. (For example, real-time systems require careful analysis of code timing, which is not part of the general-purpose IDEF0 syntax.) IDEF0 does have a special syntax designed to point to where the reader may look for further detail. This syntax is indicated at the bottom of the IDEF0 box, which is called the "mechanism side." The mechanism syntax and call-arrow syntax provide precise links between the functional and design models, but also serve the more general purpose of linking the model to other models or to other methods.

The standard way to link an IDEF0 box to another method is by means of the DRE syntax, which appears outside the box, at the lower-right corner of the box (see Figure 4-11).

If a textual expression is written in this position, it tells the reader, "Look here for further detail." This further detail may be contained in a company document describing the detailed process identified in the IDEF0 box, a military standard, the design of a mechanism that performs the function of the box, and so on. The author is encouraged to use the best, most helpful method at each step, with IDEF0 providing the high-level glue that integrates the entire system description.

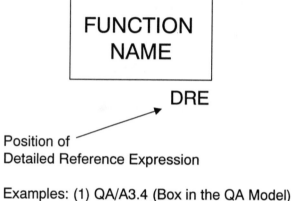

Figure 4-11: Remote Reference.

The DRE is made up of two fields, with a dot character separating the two. To the left of the dot, the node-numbering language identifies the diagram; to the right of the dot, the box number and ICOM code specify a point on the diagram. Figure 4-12 illustrates how DREs are used.

The node diagram shown at the top of Figure 4-12 identifies A4 Review & Comment as the diagram of interest. Diagram A4 appears as an inset below the node diagram, and illustrates specific DREs: If we wish to refer to box 1 on diagram A4, we write "A4.1." If we wish to refer to the second control arrow entering box 1 on diagram A4, we write "A4.1C2." To refer to the branch of the arrow that leaves box 1 and controls box 3 on diagram A4, we write "A4.1O1 to 3C2." Note that the form "A4.1O1 to 3C2" refers to the arrow branch that controls box 3, not to the branch that controls box 2. If we wish to refer to the entire arrow instead of to a single branch, we write "A4.1O1," that is, without the qualifier "to 3C2."

Node Diagram

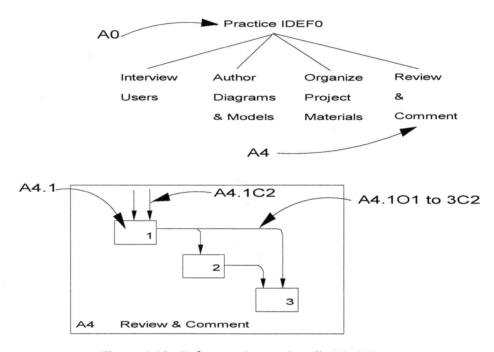

Figure 4-12: Reference Expression Illustrations.

DREs are used to link boundary arrows between diagrams within a model and between different models. They are also used wherever a concise notation is needed to refer to an item of interest in a model or diagram (such as in text or in FEO diagrams).

To link boundary arrows, a modeler annotates the lower level, or child, diagram's boundary arrows by writing the ICOM code near the unconnected end of each boundary arrow. The ICOM code refers to the position at which the boundary arrow enters or leaves the parent box from which the child diagram is decomposed. The concept is illustrated in Figure 4-13, which shows box 2 of diagram A21 (top of the figure) and its decomposition into three sub-activities in diagram A212. Two controls, one output, and one mechanism are depicted as interfaces between the child diagram and the parent box.

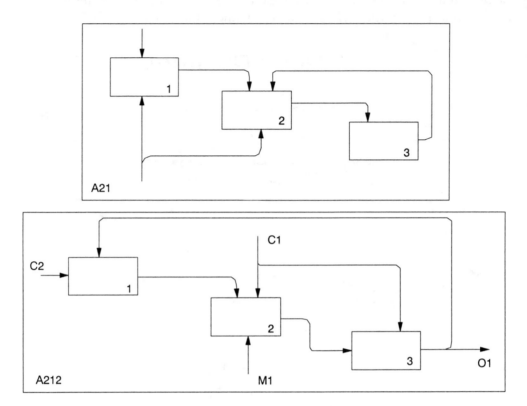

Figure 4-13: Illustration of ICOM Coding to Connect Boundary Arrows.

We have now discussed diagrams and models, including levels of detail within a model, but our discussion has not addressed the arrows used on the bottom side of the IDEF0 activity box—the mechanism side. (See Figure 4-14.)

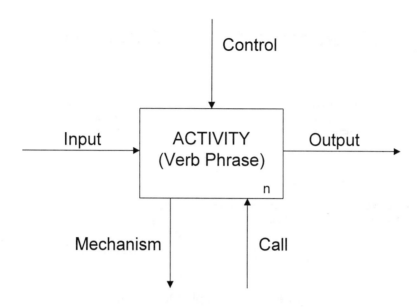

Figure 4-14: Mechanism and Call Syntax.

The primary use of the mechanism side is to show the boundary between the *what* and the *how* of enterprise activities. The mechanism side permits the analyst to consider alternative ways of implementing improvements on existing enterprise activities. Performing what is commonly called "what if" analysis, the analyst can use the mechanism to suggest a way to automate a manual process, an analysis of alternative methods at different enterprise divisions, a change in the organization structure that uses different personnel to perform an activity, an introduction of new equipment, and a variety of other what/how possibilities.

Arrows entering or leaving the bottom of the activity box indicate interfaces with the next lower level of mechanization and may be either "mechanism" arrows or "call" arrows. The entering—or mechanism—arrow represents the combination of people, equipment, and computer software that perform the activity named in the IDEF0 activity box (see Figure 4-15). The leaving—or call—arrow indicates where to look for additional detail about the activity.

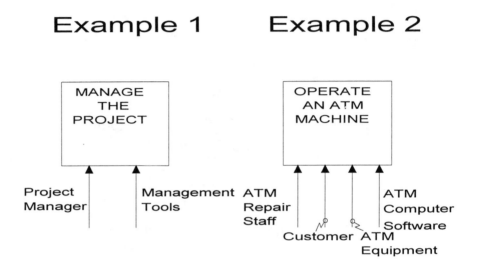

Figure 4-15: Multiple Mechanisms.

Let us first look at how the mechanism arrow functions. As we have stated, a mechanism arrow enters the bottom of the activity box. The name of the mechanism is written alongside the arrow and may be attached to the arrow by a squiggle. There is only one mechanism name per mechanism arrow, but this name may be used to designate a set of mechanisms, such as a tool set. If more than one mechanism arrow is shown entering the box, the activity is performed by a combination of the people, equipment, and software shown on the arrows (see Figure 4-15).

The set of mechanism arrows may represent how a portion—but not all—of the activity is performed. For example, the mechanism arrows included in an IDEF0 model may represent an organization, but not its equipment or computer software; this may indicate that organizational responsibility is an aspect that must be further analyzed to fulfill the purpose of the model. Or, if the support mechanisms themselves are a focus, then the equipment or computer support systems may be shown on the arrows—without showing the organizational responsibility. In a pure functional model, neither type of mechanism needs to be shown. Mechanism arrows may branch or join, just like any other IDEF0 arrow. A mechanism arrow branch indicates which mechanisms are used by which activities on the decomposition diagram. (See Figure 4-16.)

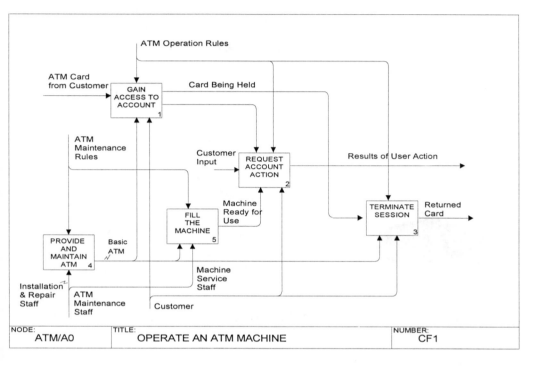

Figure 4-16: Mechanism Arrow Branching.

As we have seen, there is a second type of arrow used at the mechanism side of an activity box—the call arrow, which leaves the bottom of the box and points in the opposite direction of the mechanism arrow (see Figure 4-17). The call arrow represents a break in the activity decomposition structure, and the name written alongside the call arrow indicates where further detail about the activity can be found. For example, the call arrow might indicate a paragraph or page number in a document (such as a military standard or a company's operating procedures manual), or it may point to a full-blown IDEF0 model or to an activity box in another IDEF0 model that provides detail about the activity.

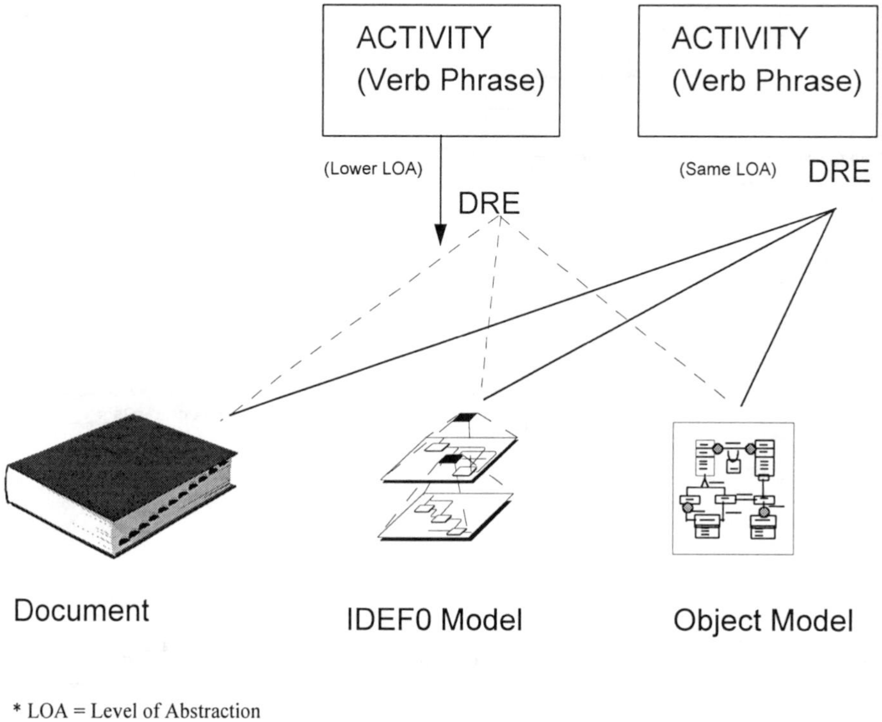

Figure 4-17: Call Points to Further Detail.

In practice, an IDEF0 author occasionally comes upon an activity that was previously encountered in the course of decomposing a parent activity. For example, two different offices may share technical publications support, a copy service, a facilities maintenance staff, and so on. These identical activities need not be modeled redundantly. Likewise, their diagrams need not be copied and reproduced multiple times in the model decomposition. Instead, the diagrams representing the redundant activity are placed in a separate model and then referenced via a call arrow at each point in the main model where the parent activity occurs (see Figure 4-18). This structure is called a many-to-one structure join, since many calls reference one model.

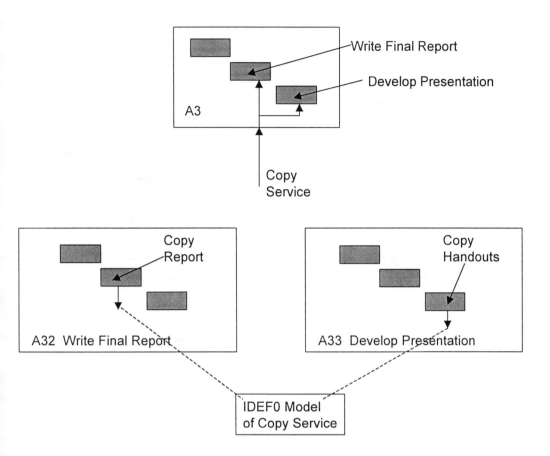

Figure 4-18: Multiple Calls to a Common Model.

In the simplest situation, the arrows entering and leaving all caller boxes are identical in number. However, this may not always be the case. That is, one or more called boxes may have a different number of input, control, or output arrows. An additional arrow most frequently indicates a parameter in the call that has an assumed or default value in the other cases. This parameter may be specified in the model by making the call arrow reference a different A-0 (single box) diagram than the actual top of the common model. The intervening A-0 diagram documents the difference between the additional arrow and the normal call by showing any additional arrows (with their default values listed in a label alongside the arrow) and an X at the unconnected end of the arrow (to indicate that it may not appear in the calling box). See Figure 4-19.

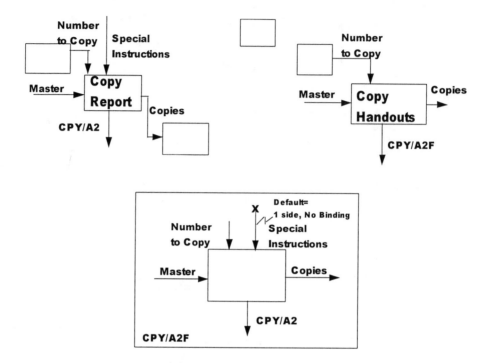

Figure 4-19: Default Values at Model Interfaces.

The split-by-type (SBT) structure shown in Figure 4-20 represents a one-to-many split—just the opposite of the previous case. That is, a single box in a decomposition calls one of a set of many equivalent activities at a lower level of abstraction. This event could be modeled as a normal child diagram, except the breakdown is not a decomposition but, rather, is an SBT structure.

Many examples of SBT occur in modeling business processes. In a manufacturing operation, for example, the point at which a manufacturing process is applied to a part is such an instance. Instead of modeling how all forms of processing are done (decomposing the verb "process"), the author decides that it would be more helpful to talk about different types of processes (see Figure 4-20).

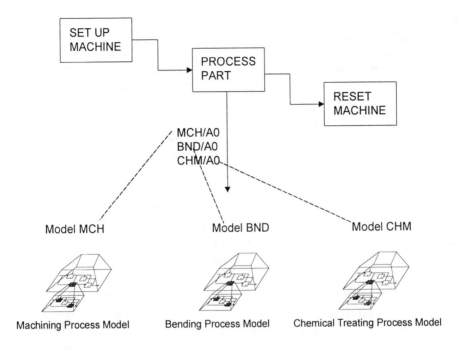

Figure 4-20: Call to Separate Process Models.

In such a case, the author would list multiple target models alongside the call arrow to indicate that any of these activities may occur at this point in the processing, depending on the content of one or more of the input or control arrows. In the manufacturing example just cited, this might be the list of instructions to the machine operator or robot, indicating which process to apply in what order.

The call arrow stems from a computer programming practice in which a subroutine may be called by a main program to accomplish a task. For example, a call might be made to a file read/write package to write a record onto a disk. The read/write package is the mechanism, whereas the write subroutine piece of the package is called to write a specific record onto the disk.

In computer programming, the subroutine call has the same effect as if the instructions in the subroutine were included at the point of the call. Since the call may occur at several locations in the main program, the size of the program's code is reduced by eliminating the need for repeating the instructions at each call location. This is analogous to the call arrow in IDEF0, in that the activity box represents the subroutine call, and the called model or document is equivalent to the entire body of the called model or document at the point of the call.

A call arrow is used at a lower level of detail than a mechanism arrow. That is, a mechanism arrow indicates that the mechanism is used to perform one or more of the sub-activities, sub-sub-activities, and so on, of the parent box on which the mechanism arrow appears. A call arrow, on the other hand, represents a precise call to a unique activity box or other form of description that matches the activity precisely. Thus, there can only be one call arrow leaving an IDEF0 box, whereas there may be many mechanism arrows entering the same box.

As we have said, a mechanism arrow may represent a person or a group of people (that is, a lone manager or the entire department staff, for example), a machine (for example, a PC or a machine tool), or a support system (a word processor, a spreadsheet system, or the like). However, since a person or machine cannot precisely match an activity, only an element of a "person," "machine," or "support system" mechanism may appear on a call arrow. Looking at the issue another way, we might say that a called activity represents a mechanism view (the *how)* of the functional description (the *what)* represented by the caller activity box.

In particular, a mechanism arrow for a software support system may be related to one or more call arrows, since the mechanism arrow may indicate general support at a higher level of detail in an IDEF0 model, and then may identify precise subsystem calls to the more detailed levels. These calls may or may not appear, depending on whether the IDEF0 model is decomposed into fine enough detail to identify specific calls. By looking again at Figure 4-18, we can see the Copy Service mechanism supporting diagram A3. The decomposition of A3 shows the copy service mechanism branching to support two sub-activities: Write Final Report (A32) and Develop Presentation (A33). The decomposition of these two activities then shows explicit calls on the copy service model from A322 and A333 for obtaining report and handout copies, respectively.

Figure 4-21 shows the mechanism- and call-arrow structure for the general-level mechanism and its corresponding calls at the detailed level. Of course, many variations are possible. There may be several levels of mechanism arrow structure before any calls appear; or there may be call and mechanism arrows that appear at the same level.

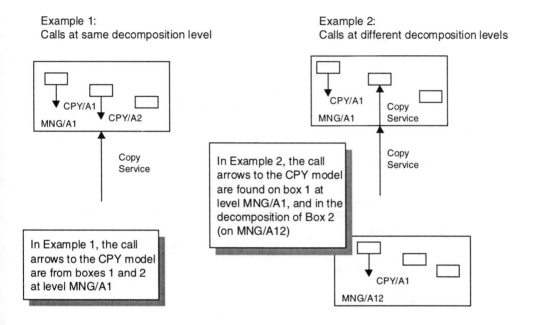

Example 1:
Calls at same decomposition level

Example 2:
Calls at different decomposition levels

CPY/A1

CPY/A2

MNG/A1

Copy
Service

CPY/A1

Copy
Service

MNG/A1

Copy
Service

In Example 1, the call
arrows to the CPY model
are from boxes 1 and 2
at level MNG/A1

In Example 2, the call
arrows to the CPY model
are found on box 1 at
level MNG/A1, and in the
decomposition of Box 2
(on MNG/A12)

CPY/A1

MNG/A12

Figure 4-21: Examples of Mechanism and Call Combinations.

Now that the role of the call arrow has been described, there may be a question as to the use of the call arrow versus the DRE, which is written below the right-hand corner of the activity box to indicate that further detail exists. The basic difference is that the DRE indicates that further detail exists at the same level of mechanization as the parent box, whereas the call arrow indicates a drop in the level of mechanization (from the functional level to the mechanism level). Figure 4-22 illustrates the difference.

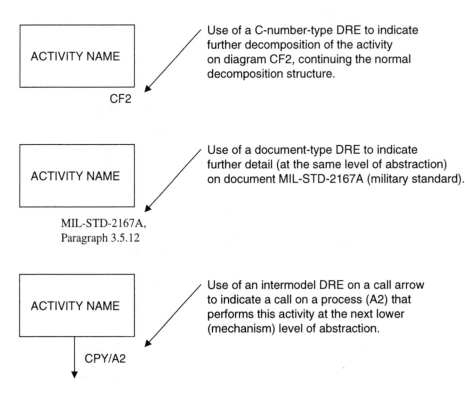

Figure 4-22: Examples of DRE and Call Arrow Use.

Recall that, in the previous example of redundant calls on the copy service, the use of a call arrow was correct, since this is a drop in level of mechanization (between the main operation of the office and the operation of the copy support service). If the redundant activity boxes had been at the same level of mechanization (two or more identical activities at the same office operations level), then a DRE below the right-hand side of the activity boxes referencing a model of the activity would have been correct (with no use of the call arrow, since a drop in level of mechanization is not indicated).

In the following chapter, we apply what we know about the syntax and semantics of IDEF0 to a higher level of modeling: *pragmatics,* or the *way* we create an IDEF0 model.

CHAPTER 5   **Pragmatics**

A s defined in *Webster's Ninth New Collegiate Dictionary*, pragmatics is a branch of semiotics that "deals with the relation between signs or linguistic expressions and their users." As used here, pragmatics governs the use of the syntax and semantics of IDEF0 to analyze an enterprise. It includes all aspects of the IDEF0 method besides its basic syntax and semantics: the rules and procedures for the application of IDEF0 that make it practical and useful.

Many modeling methods do not include a standard for pragmatics. For example, according to the IDEF1X information modeling method, as long as the IDEF1X model matches the defined syntax and semantics of the IDEF1X graphics, it is unimportant how the user of the method went about developing the model. Because IDEF0 pragmatics are so important to its successful use, I devote this entire chapter to it. Appendix E also provides a brief step-by-step example of the correct IDEF0 pragmatics for developing diagrams.

The primary elements of IDEF0 pragmatics are

- Starting an enterprise analysis with IDEF0:

    - Organize an IDEF0 enterprise analysis project.
    - Define personnel roles on a project.
    - Select proper modeling parameters: purpose, viewpoint, and type of breakdown.

- Authoring an IDEF0 model:

  - Develop interviewing techniques to extract accurate facts.
  - Balance diagrams, including clustering activities and bundling arrows.
  - Follow basic graphics layout rules for good communication.
  - Lay out the main path and secondary paths.
  - Validate the diagram using mentally simulated enterprise events.
  - Pick the next activity to decompose.
  - Stop the modeling process.

- Modeling peer reviews and critiques:

  - Employ the reader/author review cycle.
  - Conduct walkthrough sessions.

- Presenting IDEF0 models to an audience:

  - Use FEOs.
  - Use schematics.
  - Format the model for publication.

- Preparing an analysis of change impact to control implementation of improvements.

Defining the Purpose, Viewpoint, and Type of Breakdown

The step-by-step procedure for developing an IDEF0 model begins at the point at which the author determines the model parameters, that is, the purpose, viewpoint, and type of breakdown. The purpose and viewpoint must be kept constantly in mind by an IDEF0 author as he creates a model. First is purpose. The reason for creating a model is selected and then documented on the A-0 diagram at the very start of the modeling effort. A useful way for a modeler to identify the purpose is to start with the expected benefits, and then to write down how the model will achieve each benefit. The model's purpose is formally documented by completing the sentence, "The model will be used to . . . " This purpose statement can be reexamined throughout the modeling effort to ensure that the author is continuing to model relevant detail.

Second is viewpoint: the perspective of the model itself. The model's viewpoint may or may not be from the same perspective as the audience's, and it is very unlikely that it is from the same perspective as the author's. The model's viewpoint is that through which the modeled facts are filtered to provide emphasis and to present the predominant perspective of the system. For example, if the author is interested in the financial perspective of the system, then the viewpoint is financial. Likewise, a management or technical perspective may be used. In each case, the entire system is modeled in its entirety, but facts that are of most interest from the selected perspective are emphasized, while facts that are less relevant are pushed down as details to be included at a low level or not at all. The author must understand whose viewpoint is being used for the modeling and must stick to this single view throughout development of the model.

Whenever I explain to students what is meant by viewpoint, someone will claim that each person in the world has a unique viewpoint—the way he sees things, what he is interested in, what his goals are, what he considers important. This is true, but such an outlook does not help an IDEF0 author determine viewpoint. What *is* useful is the knowledge that people often can be classified as to type of job (such as accountant, secretary, or programmer), and it is this classification that helps determine IDEF0 viewpoints. People with business school degrees may be said to have a background in business or finance, for example; people who had college majors in mathematics, physics, or computer science may be said to have a technical view; people who manage a project may be said to have a project manager's view; and so on. In other words, the model's viewpoint is related to the grouping of viewpoints associated with the job to be accomplished.

Viewpoint is critical to proper model communication. It is logical, therefore, that if a financial viewpoint is selected, then financial terminology (general ledgers, cost accounts, return on investment) should be used to capture the picture. A technician looking at a financial-view model might not completely understand the jargon, but the jargon is necessary in order to communicate the model to people who have a financial background. Mixing viewpoints within a single model destroys the clarity of the model.

Viewpoint and audience are not identical, and should not be thought of as such by a modeler. A financial model, for example, may adopt a specific viewpoint that is different from that of its management audience. However, the viewpoint of all readers checking model accuracy and completeness during the reader/author critique cycle must match the model's viewpoint, or they will not be qualified to provide a proper critique of the facts.

In addition to purpose and viewpoint, the third parameter that must be decided before modeling begins is what type of breakdown to select. Consideration of this parameter is sometimes omitted by practitioners of IDEF0, since SADT allowed only one type of activity (functional) and one form of breakdown (decomposition). There are other types of activity and other forms of breakdown, but for purposes of this book, the two values of functional activity and decomposition will be used here. (See Appendix A for a discussion of these other forms of activity and how they may be selected to model specific systems for selected purposes.)

Before modeling can begin, the project must be staffed, and agreements must be established defining how much modeling support will be provided from a broad range of personnel. Table 5.1 summarizes the roles of the various staff who must be involved in an IDEF0 project.

Table 5-1.
IDEF0 Project Personnel.

ROLE	RESPONSIBILITY
Author	Creates models from documents and conducts interviews with experts
Expert	Provides information to authors
Reader	Reviews models
Commenter	Reviews and critiques models
Review Committee	Approves models for specific approval levels (working, draft, and publication levels)
Librarian	Manages the master files, controls the reader/author kit process, and provides management reports

As part of starting the project, and author needs to establish agreements governing how much interview time will be required from experts, how much review time will come from commenters, and which group leaders and managers will serve on the review committee. Typically, there is one lead author and from one to four additional authors on a project. The reason for this is that if there were only one author, he would have no other knowledgeable IDEF0 person to review and critique his working level and draft diagrams, but if there were too many authors, assignments would become unwieldy and hard to coordinate.

Starting the Model

Once the model's parameters have been determined and documented and the staffing issues settled, the authors are ready to start modeling. The author with the most experience is identified as the lead author and is typically responsible for developing the A-0 diagram, as well as for decomposing the most complicated activities during model development. As we have already noted (see Figure 4-4 in Chapter 4), all diagrams in IDEF0, as well as all text, glossary entries, node diagrams, and FEOs, are written onto a single form: the IDEF0 diagram form.

At the outset, authors should study any existing documentation for the system to be modeled. In most cases, this documentation either is out of date or does not exist at all, and so most of the real information is obtained during interviews with the system experts. The interview process begins with the authors putting the user expert at ease by providing an introduction to the IDEF0 method, followed by a brief overview of the project and a description of the kind of information that is sought.

Once this introductory session has been finished, the authors should turn the conversation over to the expert, asking him to describe the process to be modeled and making sure that the description comes entirely from the expert's viewpoint. Author interviewers should interrupt only if they are confused—typically, to define an unknown term or an apparent conflict in the story—keeping in mind that too much directing of the conversation by an interviewer will impose his viewpoint on the story and unduly influence the expert.

The end of the interview occurs either when the expert has said everything he wishes to about the subject or when roughly two hours have passed. At this point, the lead author thanks the expert and tells him that he will model the results of the interview and will return to verify the resultant diagrams by walking the expert through the model. The purpose for the walkthrough is to confirm that the authors have understood correctly, and that they have not left out important details or overemphasized something unimportant.

After the conclusion of the first interview but before another interview occurs, the lead author needs to analyze the interview notes and sketch out a first working-level diagram that captures the information gathered. When a diagram is first drawn by an author, it is considered to be at working level. For a diagram to progress from working level to draft level, it must go through a reader review by one or two other authors. This review should catch obvious errors and should ensure that the basic concepts and method are applied correctly.

Timing is crucial. If the interview note-review process is delayed, the information will become less meaningful and misunderstandings may creep in. Drafting diagrams *during* the interview has not proven to be practical for most authors, since facts usually are provided in a disorganized sequence and may be clouded by irrelevant side remarks.

The first task for the author reviewing the interview notes is to make a data list of all things mentioned during the interview. The list identifies the primary elements of data—resources, people, raw materials, and so on—that are used and created by the system to be modeled. This list will most likely consist of twenty to thirty items, some of which are self-contained and some of which are related to others. The next step is to bundle these items into groups, such as types of plans, instructions, reports, financial data, and the like. Groupings should be made up of similar kinds of items that can be bundled, like wires in an electrical conduit, and then passed along to other activities that will make use of them.

After listing and bundling the data, the lead author is ready to focus on the activities themselves by considering which ones either use or produce the data in the bundled data list. Once the list of activities includes either production of or use of all data items on the list, the author can be confident that he has completed the task.

Topics mentioned by the expert in the interview should now be cross-checked with the newly created usage-based activity list to see that there are no holes, either in activity or in data elements identified. As we have discussed, the maximum number of activities permitted on a single IDEF0 diagram is six, so if more than six activities result from this effort, they should be clustered into more general activities that encompass an entire set.

Finally, the set of activities must be split and re-clustered based on level of complexity. That is, if one or two activities are simpler to accomplish than the others, the resultant diagram will not be balanced. Some activities will be hard to understand, while others will be very simple and uninteresting.

Once six or fewer categories of activities have been identified and named, and once all activities and data mentioned in the interview are included somewhere, the author lays out his first diagram draft. The diagram follows a staircase layout, with those activities generating the most outputs placed toward the upper left of the diagram. It is important to note that action sequence is not a factor in laying out a diagram. An activity that must operate first is not necessarily in the upper-left activity box, because IDEF0 diagrams are intended to show constraint and dominance rather than sequence.

When the activity box layout is complete, the author can add arrow pathways to the diagram. Figure 5-1 illustrates the arrow layout rules of IDEF0.

To add the arrow pathways, the author draws the main path arrows first, showing the typical way the activities on the diagram will operate if no unusual events occur. This main path is usually generated by the author's mentally simulating the action of the diagram's parent box. As each input, output, and activation of a new box occurs, the author adds arrows for whatever inputs and controls are needed by the activity box.

Once the main path is complete, the author examines each box to determine alternative behavior and feedback that represent the adaptability of the system. In this effort, the author needs to consider how the system reacts to faulty data or error conditions that may occur. This consideration typically causes the number of arrows to increase significantly. If the complexity becomes too great and the draft becomes cluttered, the author should redraw the draft diagram before presenting it to the expert for review.

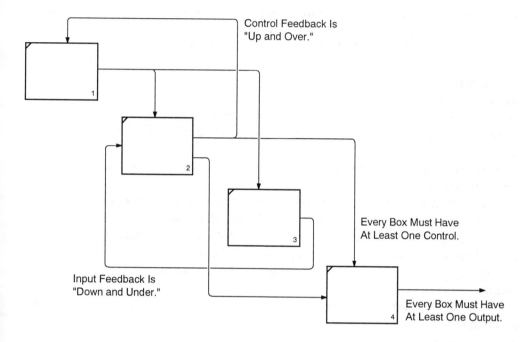

Figure 5-1: Arrow Layout Rules.

A rule to keep in mind when adding an arrow is: *When in doubt, leave it out.* That is, if you are not sure that the information (or material, software, equipment, signal, and so on) provided by an arrow is needed by an activity, then do not draw the arrow. The decomposition process should reveal whether the arrow is really needed.

When all arrow pathways have been added to the diagram, the author must check to see that each arrow is properly labeled. As is true with fork/joins, arrow segments need not be labeled if the name of the main branch is also appropriate for each segment branch. However, if a subset of the *entire* arrow content is really what is used, a constraining label should be added to each arrow branch to make the diagram more precise.

The author must also check to see that he has not accidentally labeled two distinct arrow segments with the identical label. If identical labels are discovered, the author must add a modifier appropriate to one or the other label to make the two distinct. For example, the label "requirements" may be more precisely identified as "user requirements" or "management requirements."

Oddly, some new IDEF0 authors label input arrows very well but neglect to label control arrows precisely. The model therefore winds up with a set of "fat" all-encompassing arrows controlling very small activities at the bottom of the model. For example, "rules and regulations" would be found controlling a detailed activity, instead of indicating which specific rules and regulations apply.

As the final step during this labeling phase, the authors must define what is on each arrow and record each definition in the model glossary. It is at this point in the diagramming effort that the author is most familiar with what he intended to bundle into his large pipeline arrows, and he can record precise pipeline contents while these details are fresh in his mind. If he waits until later in the cycle, he may not remember all of the elements of the pipeline. The model glossary will also be useful to subsequent readers, who might misinterpret an arrow if they cannot look up what is intended.

Glossary-generating tools may be useful in the diagramming effort and, in fact, some IDEF0 computer packages include a facility that enables the user to call for a glossary page for any selected diagram. The tool creates a separate glossary dia-gram field for *each* arrow label that appears on the diagram. Using this field as a prompt, the author may easily run through a set of arrow definitions to capture his intent.

Once the glossary has been completed, the author should recheck the diagram to see that it accurately represents his understanding of the facts. To check the dia-gram, the author may wish to postulate a series of scenarios simulating the action depicted in the diagram. This simulation might consist of the author "feeding" a series of initial conditions to the model to see how it handles each case. Once this "sanity check" has been performed, the author can turn the diagram over to the project librarian for distribution in the form of a reader kit, and can be well satis-fied that the job of creating the first-draft IDEF0 diagram is complete.

Validating the Model

Although finished with the diagram draft, the author cannot afford to wait for a response from the commenters before continuing the modeling effort. His next task is to examine the diagram and to pick a box for decomposition. It is impor-tant for the efficiency of the IDEF0 project that the author pick the correct box. The choice should not necessarily be the most complex box or the box that the author knows most about, but rather the box that will reveal the most new information. Typically, this is the box that the author knows least about. Decomposition of it will help the author determine whether he has omitted anything from the model, or has misunderstood something. If an error or omission is not discovered early, the author may waste considerable effort pursuing a misunderstanding, and the activity will have to be remodeled later.

After questions, suggestions for change, and any error notations about the first and revised draft diagrams have come back from the commenters, and after the full set of diagrams in the model has been validated through the reader/author cycle process, text is written to accompany each diagram. This text must not be written during the diagram-creation process, since there is a danger that the author may include facts in the text as a substitute for changing the diagram to include those facts. The diagram by itself must represent the entire model of the topic. The text should not attempt to tell the reader every fact that can be seen by reading the diagram; nor should it be a description of what is contained in the future decomposition of the boxes on the diagram.

Diagram text is best used to discuss boxes and arrows that illustrate the handling of a typical case or that represent a key role by a staff member. However, diagram text is not restricted to this type of discussion; it is open-ended, allowing the author to highlight whatever is important about the diagram (see Figure 5-2 for an illustration of a highlighted diagram).

Once the full model and diagram text have been approved by the designated technical committee and the approval box on each diagram form has been signed, the whole is formatted for publication, printed, and distributed. Publication format for an IDEF0 model includes a reduced-size copy of the parent diagram on which the parent box is highlighted by color, gray tint, or shading. This reduced-size diagram is placed in the upper-right corner of the page, which is printed in landscape (not portrait) orientation, and the text for the diagram annotates the remainder of the page (snaking to the left and below the parent diagram). The full-size parent diagram is reproduced on the facing page (see Figure 5-3), with its header field missing. The C-numbers below any boxes that are decomposed are replaced with the page number in the published model document. Following is an example of a single publication-format diagram, with text.

MOD/A2 AUTHOR DIAGRAMS AND MODELS

This modeling process is where diagrams are created. The primary modeling steps for IDEF0 are presented as boxes 1 to 5. Box 1 includes reading and refining information from documents and notes resulting from initial interviews (box 1 of the parent). The expert is shown as a mechanism to box 1 to indicate that he will be needed to verify facts, explain things that were unclear in the initial notes (1I1), and provide additional information that comes to mind now that the detailed decomposition of the subject is being authored. Note that the standard stairstep layout is used except for box 6. Box 6 is presented below the stairstep structure to indicate that it is a process of reacting to reader comments and not part of the main diagram generation process.

Boxes 2 and 3 are steps that are sometimes skipped by authors who are in a hurry. However, these steps ensure that the decomposition form of breakdown is followed, instead of one of the other possible forms. A key point that illustrates the use of the data clusters in formulating the list of activities for the diagram is shown at 2O1 to 3C1. Here, the data clusters are not changed in box 3, but serve to control the selection of the activities that make up the diagram.

The diagram shows not only the initial diagramming process but also the change process resulting from using scenarios as walkthrough tests (box 5), as well as the handling of the revisions to the model due to the reader/author (R/A) cycle critique (box 6). The accepted changes (6O1) are handled just like any changes resulting from the scenario evaluation (box 5) validation. That is, they are fed back to cause the diagram layout to be changed (box 4) or for major reclustering and rebundling in box 3. Rejected changes are not shown explicitly since they are passed back to the reader as part of the kits with author responses (6O2).

The diagram indicates that reminders from the librarian (C2) are used only to control the author response to readers. Since this control does not appear on box 1, this indicates that the librarian is not responsible for seeing that the author does his initial modeling tasks on time, but only that he does not hold up the R/A cycle process.

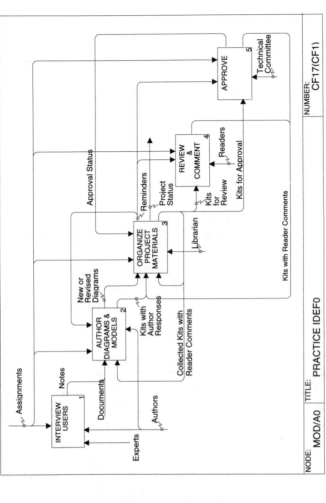

NODE:	TITLE:	NUMBER:
MOD/A0	PRACTICE IDEF0	CF17/CF1

Figure 5-2: A Highlighted Diagram.

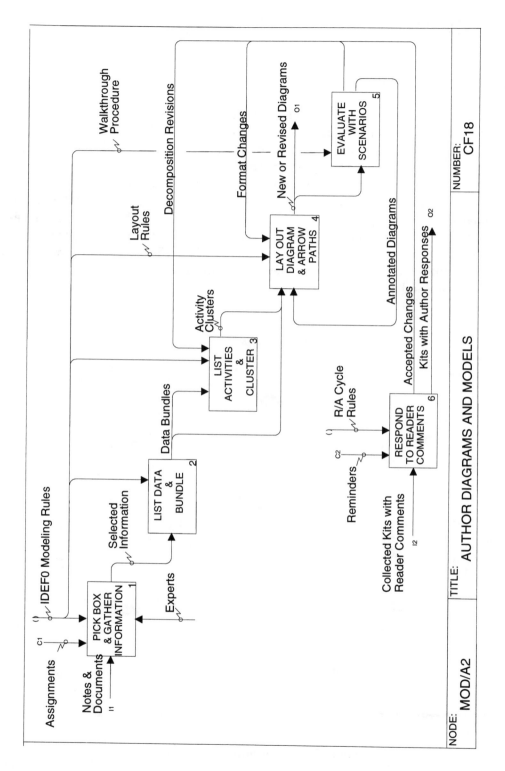

Figure 5-3: A Publication Format Diagram.

Modeling Other Viewpoints

To cover all important aspects of a system, the author may need to create several models from different viewpoints. However, these models are not necessarily independent; activities from one viewpoint sometimes relate to activities from a different viewpoint. For example, a report drawn from the technical viewpoint might record how many hours were spent by each worker each day on a particular task, but the information might also need to be reported at regular intervals to management. This represents an intersection between the technical and management viewpoints and indicates that the staff working from one viewpoint must interact with the staff from another viewpoint. Figure 5-4 illustrates a model in which technical and management viewpoints are tied while the financial viewpoint remains independent.

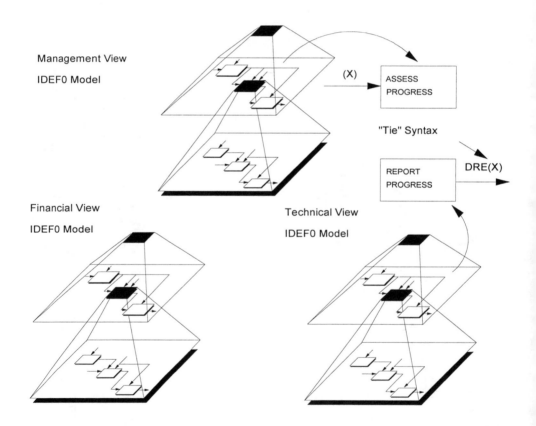

Figure 5-4: Intermodel Tie Syntax.

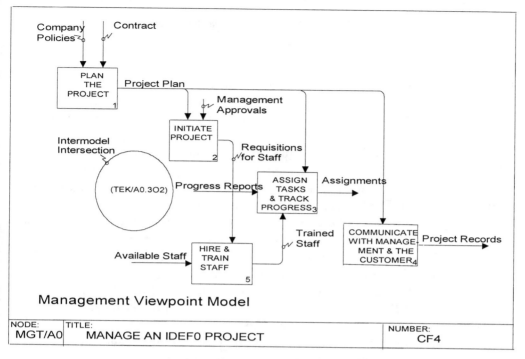

Figure 5-5: Management Viewpoint Model.

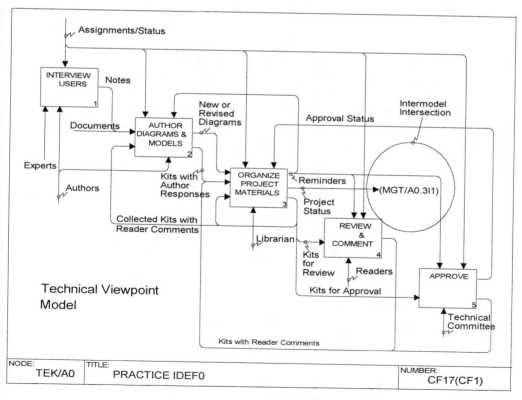

Figure 5-6: Technical Viewpoint Model.

Intersections between two models from different viewpoints must exist as activity boxes in both models. As shown in Figure 5-4, arrows passing information back and forth between two viewpoints are connected using a DRE reference at the end of each unconnected boundary arrow.

Figures 5-5 and 5-6 show the occurrence of an intermodel intersection. Figure 5-5 contains the A0 diagram of the management viewpoint (model name MGT). Box 3, ASSIGN TASKS & TRACK PROGRESS, has an intersection with the technical viewpoint (model name TEK). What Figure 5-6 shows is that, on a regular basis, the librarian reports the status of the reader/author cycle to the project manager (output 2 of box 3). This arrow (3O2) indicates an interface from the technical viewpoint to the management viewpoint. The DRE at the head of arrow 3O2 identifies the point at which the data is received by the management viewpoint activity (MGT/A0.3I1). In Figure 5-5, the unconnected arrow tail into box 3 is labeled TEK/A0.3O2 to indicate that the source of this data is in the technical viewpoint model, diagram A0, third box, second output.

In the preceding example, and in any case in which various viewpoints intersect, multiple models at the *same* level of abstraction are linked using the DRE language to pinpoint intermodel connection points. In any case in which two *different* levels of abstraction (integrating multiple viewpoint models) are linked, the call arrow syntax is used to indicate that the decomposition from the present level of abstraction is complete and that further details are to be found at the next lower level of abstraction. This form of level x to level $x+1$ connection is illustrated in Figure 5-7, which depicts a situation in which the author has decided that it is no longer useful to model the activity report on finances in general, preferring instead to model specific types of reports: RPT1, RPT2, RPT3. As in the previous example of inter-viewpoint model intersection, the DRE notation is used to identify the specific point in the model referenced alongside the call arrow. In this case, the DRE identifies the box in the called model that corresponds to the calling box (REPORT ON FINANCES).

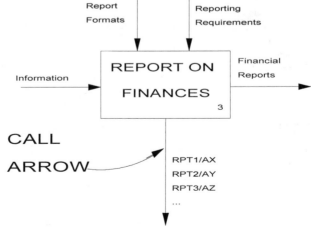

Figure 5-7: Call Arrow Illustration.

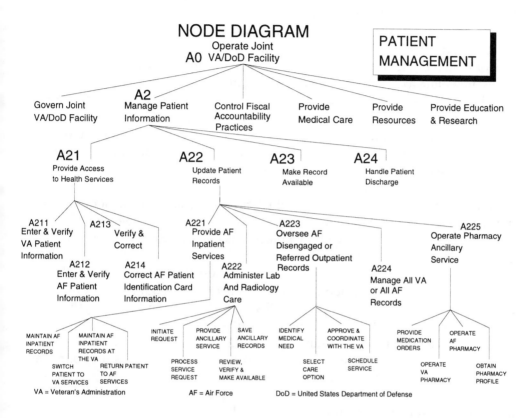

Figure 5-8: Sample Node Diagram for Communicating Model Content.

Using Node Diagrams, Schematics, and FEO Diagrams

It is critical to develop a useful model that contains the information needed to satisfy the purpose for which the model was developed. However, if the model sits on the shelf, or if the presentation of modeling results does not convey its meaning to the audience, a significant portion of the model's value will be lost.

One method of illustrating the content of the model is the *node tree*, or *node diagram*. A wall chart containing the node tree provides a very effective way to show management the breadth and depth of information contained in the model. Whenever a particular aspect of the system needs to be understood or changed, the node tree can be used to locate the specific IDEF0 diagrams that present the needed information.

Figure 5-8 shows the node tree for the patient management portion of the model of a joint Veterans Administration/Department of Defense hospital. By examining the activities in the model as shown on the node diagram, any viewer can see an overview of the content of the model, including which activities are broken down to what level of detail. For example, inspection of the node diagram in Figure 5-8 shows that activity A221 (Provide AF Inpatient Services) is broken down, but activity A24 (Handle Patient Discharge) is not further detailed in the present model. This tells the viewer that the manager can retrieve the detailed picture of Air Force inpatient handling, but the viewer would have to request further IDEF0 modeling to obtain details of how the patient discharge process works.

The node diagram facilitates communication by allowing management to sit back and contemplate the operation of the enterprise as modeled from a solid technical foundation. Furthermore, management and staff can discuss operation of the enterprise using the node diagram as a baseline, confident that they are using the same well-defined terms for specific activities.

Node diagrams are valuable, but they are not sufficient models in and of themselves; they do not constitute a true IDEF0 model. Because of the node diagram's utility to management, it is sometimes the *only* so-called model developed in some organizations. One problem with this practice is that the resultant node diagram is not based on careful analysis (that is, it is not developed using step-by-step IDEF0 procedures) and is thus not well-founded in fact. A second problem is that the node diagram alone cannot bring about the many benefits derived through development of a true IDEF0 model (for example, benefits associated with impact analysis).

Another form for presenting model results is a *schematic,* which is also the basic chart used in a model walkthrough. A schematic is developed by laying out the bottom (most detailed) level of an IDEF0 model on a large sheet of paper and then connecting the arrow pathways (see Figure 5-9). It can be helpful to color-code the types of data on the arrows. For example, use red for raw materials and product, green for controls, and yellow for feedback.

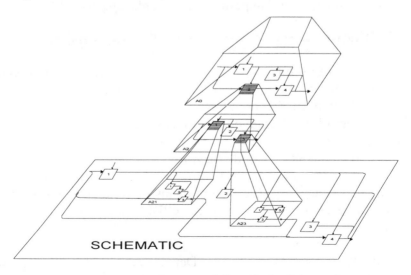

SCHEMATIC

Figure 5-9: Process of Creating a Schematic.

For a walkthrough presentation, the presenter can attach the large schematic sheet to a wall and lead the audience through it, pointing to the relevant activities or arrow paths. Further questions and conclusions may be presented as they occur, such as "Notice that since there are no yellow arrows in this vicinity, there is no feedback here. Is this correct?" Specific events to test the completeness and accuracy of the model may be proposed by the audience, developed prior to the start of the meeting, or both.

The schematic format may seem to contradict one of the basic principles of IDEF0—that information be provided in small, easy-to-understand chunks. However, a walkthrough using a schematic is by far the most effective way to lead an audience through the model so that the audience can evaluate the correctness and completeness of the model. The schematic eliminates the need for lots of paper shuffling while connecting the arrow interfaces, enabling the audience to see both ends of the interface.

A third and final form for presenting model results is the for-exposition-only (FEO) diagram (introduced in Chapter 4). On an FEO diagram, the author is not restricted by IDEF0 modeling rules. For example, more than six boxes can be shown if this is helpful in making a point. A common use of an FEO is to show a particular pathway to illustrate a specific scenario. Figure 5-10, "Practice IDEF0," could be used to train new librarians in their duties, because it highlights instances in which the librarian is called on to perform record-keeping and reporting tasks. Seven such events and their successive scenarios were developed for this training to cover the total spectrum of librarian duties.

Figure 5-10 presents one of the seven FEO diagrams in this training package. It represents the initial submission of working-level approval kits to the librarian. In the version shown, all unrelated boxes and arrows have been removed, leaving only the elements of interest to the scenario. By creating six additional FEOs, the modeler completes the set of training materials for all seven events handled by the librarian. An alternative form is to leave all boxes and arrows on the diagram but just highlight those of interest to the particular viewpoint or scenario.

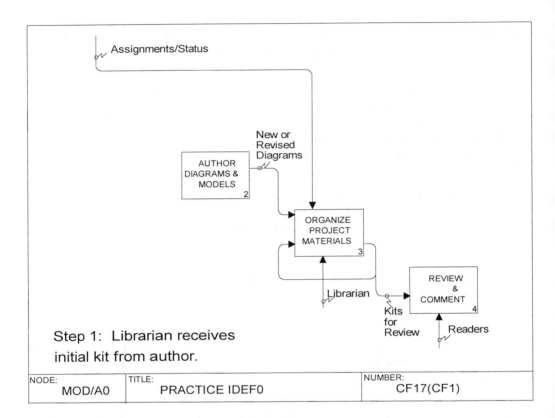

Figure 5-10: FEO Showing First Librarian Event.

The bundling and branching of arrow contents is often spread over many diagrams. This spread makes it difficult to identify arrow structure or to check the
structure for errors, such as an arrow coming out of a process that was never bundled into the pipeline arrow.

Some new software tools provide checks for this phenomenon. However,
where particularly critical arrows are involved, it may be helpful to draw an FEO
that illustrates the arrow bundling and branching picture on a single diagram
form. An illustration of such an FEO (taken from a mission-planning Gulf War
model) is shown in Figure 5-11.

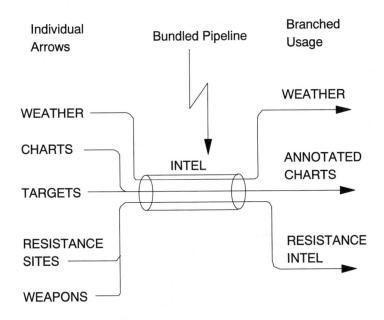

Figure 5-11: The Raveled-Rope FEO.

Looking at Figure 5-11, we see five arrows on the left side, labeled Weather, Charts, Targets, Resistance Sites, and Weapons. The five arrows are bundled into a single, large arrow in the center, labeled Intel.[1] The right side of the figure shows three arrows emerging from Intel, labeled Weather, Annotated Charts, and Resistance Intel. This FEO illustrates the content of the arrow Intel, and shows the following facts about that large arrow:

- The individual arrow Weather is contained within Intel but also emerges as Weather when it is split out as a control arrow.
- Charts and Targets are part of Intel but are also used under the label Annotated Charts when split out from Intel.
- Resistance Sites and Weapons are included in Intel and are also bundled into the arrow labeled Resistance Intel when used in the model either as an input or as a control.

The information contained in this FEO could be deciphered by a determined reader, but it might take the reader considerable time and effort to follow the Intel arrow backward to identify the arrow joins (the five individual arrows that join to

---

[1] Intel is used here to identify intelligence data used for strike planning.

form Intel), and forward to find the three places where the main Intel arrow forks and is labeled with branch labels. The search would probably involve locating and examining many individual diagrams in the model.

The value of the FEO, therefore, is that it enables a reader to identify the information about Intel at a glance. Of course, the definition of the arrow Intel in the glossary should contain the same information, but the graphic FEO form may be more helpful for purposes of immediate communication and emphasis.

Figure 5-12 shows a selected portion of a model (the A31 branch) in which the Intel pipeline is formed via several joins: Resistance Sites and Weapons on A3112, Targets on its parent diagram A311, and the final two elements (Weather and Charts) on A31. Diagram A313 shows Intel breaking down via forking into the three arrows: Annotated Charts, Weather, and Resistance Intel.

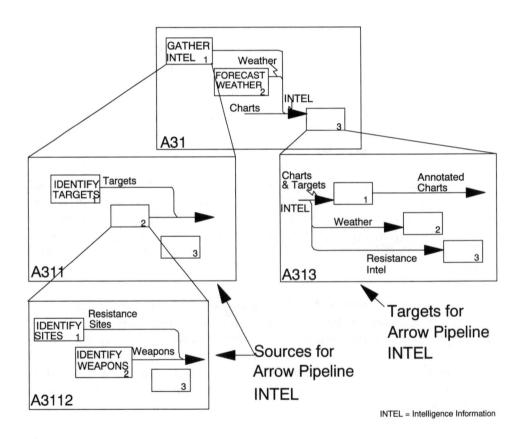

Figure 5-12: Arrow Trace Process.

Diagram A313 shows some typical arrow tracing logic. Intel is shown forking into three parts: Charts & Targets going into box 1, Weather going into box 2, and Resistance Intel going into box 3. An analysis of the Intel arrow source must conclude that Resistance Intel contains Resistance Sites and Weapons, since all other bundled Intel arrow content is accounted for. Furthermore, charts and targets appear to be combined as input into box 1 of A313. When creating the FEO, the analyst would, of course, have to look carefully at box 1 to determine whether the annotated charts are indeed comprised only of charts with targets marked on them or if the annotated charts contain other data as well.

In actual situations, arrow tracing to find sources and targets might be quite complex, and might involve locating and analyzing many diagrams to create an accurate raveled-rope FEO. The example presented here is intended simply to give the reader a feeling for the process of creating such FEOs.

These examples should serve to illustrate the use of FEOs. Any form of figure or text is permitted as an FEO to illustrate a point about the model. Other forms of FEO include timing data superimposed on the boxes and arrows, number of personnel and cost data written on the mechanism arrow, AS-IS and TO-BE variations, and so on.

Using the Reader/Author Review Process

The important difference to keep in mind between a graphical modeling language and a complete methodology is that the latter includes the procedures and tools to make proper use of the language. With IDEF0, the interview procedures, the guidelines for creating diagrams, the configuration management of models and documents, the peer review using the reader/author critique cycle, and the model walkthroughs are all essential to the successful application of the method.

A manual configuration-management procedure, including forms and records-keeping methods, was originally a part of the IDEF0 tool kit. The manual approach has been replaced by comparable facilities in each of the computerized support tools for IDEF0. Many of the support tools also provide assistance with the critique of models. This process constitutes the R/A cycle, which represents a back-and-forth communication path; its purpose is to verify and validate models and to reach consensus among the staff that needs to understand and agree with model content.

To set up a reader/author review cycle, the project manager must decide who should review what and at what point in the modeling process. Although who reviews and when is up to the project manager, the process is not. The IDEF0 method defines four levels of approval (working, draft, recommended, and publication), with a select list of readers who must reach consensus for the model to move from one level to the next higher level.

To move from one level to the next, a diagram must be reviewed and approved by an audience of a specific viewpoint. For example, to achieve *recommended* level, the diagram is assigned to a larger group of readers from different backgrounds and interests. Such people must be knowledgeable both about the system being modeled and about who will be affected if changes are implemented. Readers at this third level are not necessarily authors, but they must be committed to the modeling results.

The review committee (see Table 5-1) has final responsibility for approving the model at the publication level. This committee is made up of one or more managers who must sign off on the model before it can be published and be considered accepted. In performing this role, the technical committee has the final say on disagreements that cannot be settled by the reader/author review. Final disagreements are typically few, but they require management sign-off for the resolution of critically important modeling results.

Figure 5-13 illustrates the process of progression through approval levels, of correcting errors and omissions, and of remodeling areas of the model to improve communication and focus.

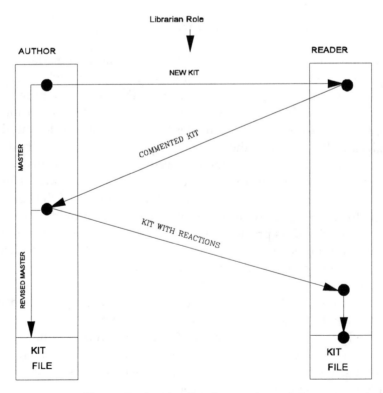

Figure 5-13: The Reader/Author Cycle.

As shown in the upper-left corner of Figure 5-13, the R/A cycle begins with the author, who generates the first version of one or more diagrams. When he is satisfied that the story being told is basically correct, he saves the master copy and creates a reader kit containing one or more working-level diagrams that he considers ready for review. This kit is copied and distributed to the list of readers for the first level of approval (shown by an arrow from upper left to upper right of the figure). Each reader then comments on the kit of diagrams, using the commenting procedure. Comments and suggestions are written on each sheet of the kit, and remarks that pertain to the entire kit are noted on the cover sheet (see Figure 5-14). Readers then return their marked-up kits to the author.

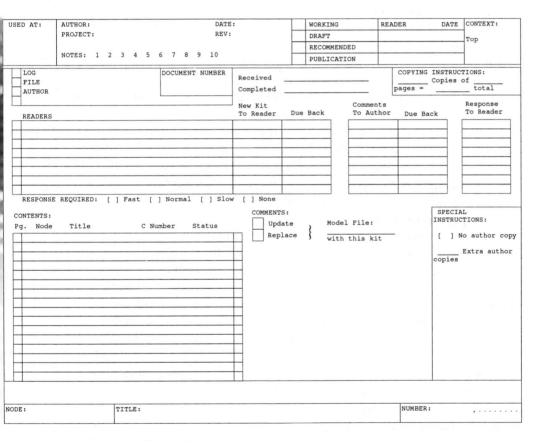

Figure 5-14: The Reader Kit Cover Sheet.

The author reviews and responds to each comment from each reader. Suggestions that the author decides to accept are written on a clean copy of the kit and are used to prepare the revised master of the diagrams. The kits with reader comments and author responses are then sent back to the readers for their information (left center to lower right of Figure 5-13). When each reader receives his kit with responses from the author, he reviews individual comments and responses. Those responses he disagrees with are noted, to be resolved in a subsequent meeting with the author. Each reader then files the marked-up kit for reference when the updated kit of diagrams is distributed at a later date. This completes one round of the reader/author cycle.

The author begins the second round by updating the master copy of the diagrams and distributing a second kit containing the revised diagrams to the same set of readers. This time, readers compare their marked-up kits from the previous round to check changes made in response to the set of suggested improvements.

The reader/author cycle continues until consensus is achieved on all diagrams. If disagreements remain between the author and one or more of the readers, this is resolved at a meeting of the technical committee. When all issues are resolved, the diagrams in the kit are raised to the next appropriate approval level by marking the box in the upper-right corner of the diagram form. The next reader/author cycle is then begun, to achieve the next level of approval, until the publication level of approval is achieved.

The kit cover sheet used in reader kit processing is patterned after the diagram form in that both have identical header and footer pieces. The information field found at the center of the page of a diagram is replaced on the kit cover sheet by the information needed to move the kit through the reader/author cycle.

The project librarian is responsible for keeping track of the kit cycle and therefore keeps the cover sheet updated. When a kit of diagrams is received from an author, the librarian assigns it a unique document number, writes the number in the designated box at the top of the form, enters the date the kit was received, and authorizes copies to be made for the desired set of readers.

Readers are selected by the IDEF0 manager prior to distribution of any kits. When a kit is received, the readers' names are written in a column on the top-left side of the cover sheet. The urgency of the response (fast, normal, or slow) or the fact that no response is required is checked off, according to project policy. ("Fast" may vary from a few hours to a week, depending on the geographical location and availability of the readers.) The librarian enters dates and times into the fields to the right of the names, as the cycle progresses.

The node number, title, C-number, and status of each sheet is entered into the contents column at the lower-left quadrant of the cover sheet. The preprinted letter corresponding to each sheet in the kit is then copied from the left side of the contents field and then entered in the small dotted rectangle at the extreme lower-right corner of each page.

Many of the mechanical kit-processing tasks are now supported by the same computer tools that are used to generate IDEF0 models themselves. Where automated kit processing is available, an electronic version of the kit cover sheet is used. The tool supports kit preparation by automatically filling many of the fields on the kit cover sheet. For example, the author's name, the date, and the document number may be supplied automatically when the author calls for the generation of a kit. Diagrams to be included in the kit may be selected by the point-and-click method, using the node index. If the tool is connected to a network, support often includes sending kit copies through the network to each of the readers and receiving back comments via the same network.

The reader/author kit cycle is the key peer-review process of IDEF0. The project manager of a BPR project that uses IDEF0 should take into account this aspect of tool support when determining which tool to purchase in conjunction with his IDEF0 modeling effort.

The reader/author cycle is the least expensive form of review and requires the least amount of management overhead time, since each reader may review the kit on his own schedule, thus relieving management from the task of organizing review meetings. Readers are given due-date schedules on the kit cover sheet, specifying when the comments are due to the author. Similarly, the author has a due date for his responses to the readers. However, this schedule depends on an honor system among the readers and authors, which sometimes breaks down. The breakdown is not necessarily due to negligence, but rather to many other potential delays and conflicts. To break any such logjams, a back-up walkthrough procedure is used. The walkthrough procedure is simply a step-by-step presentation of each diagram to an audience of readers. It provides a thorough examination of the diagrams in an orderly, prescribed way. The goal is to uncover oversights and errors in the diagrams as the readers follow the story being told via the walkthrough.

Of course, the walkthrough procedure is an approach to presenting an IDEF0 model to an audience in general. In some cases, the audience may not be trained readers of IDEF0 models, and more care must be taken to present basic reading rules at the outset of the walkthrough meeting. In other cases, it may be preferable to convert the model facts into a different presentation form (schematics, bar charts, and so on) to match the level of abstraction of the audience.

Do's and Don'ts

CHAPTER 6

The previous chapters define the IDEF0 method in terms of its concepts, its language, and its pragmatics. To be considered formal, any method needs to have a documented set of rules that must be obeyed, and IDEF0 has proven itself to be a formal method. For example, one IDEF0 syntax rule is that there may not be more than six activities on a diagram; a semantics rule is that a label on an arrow branch restricts the flow of data on that branch; and a pragmatics rule is that the arrows on a diagram should be bundled to match the level of detail of the activities on that diagram.

Since the formal elements of the IDEF0 method have thus been defined above, this book could end here and be a complete description of IDEF0. However, the experience of analysts applying SADT and IDEF0 during the past twenty years have revealed numerous misuses of the method—misuses that are instructive and that, when studied, should be helpful to every user of IDEF0. Misuses are presented in this final chapter with the hope that awareness of them will help future IDEF0 analysts avoid them.

There are many *do's and don'ts*—the list seems almost endless. In this chapter, I set down the most common ones from my experience, organizing them into three categories: language rules, model quality (quality measurements and subjective assessment recommendations), and modeling project management issues.

Language Rules

As a starting point, let's take a look at the IDEF0 language rules that apply to boxes, arrows, diagrams, and models (summarized in Table 6-1), especially in terms of specific misuses of the IDEF0 method, problems that result from each misuse, and ways to correct or avoid each problem.

Table 6-1.
Summary of IDEF0 Rules.

BOX RULES:
(1) Single-digit box number appears in lower-right corner.
(2) All activities have at least one control and one output.
(3) Each box has a name consisting of a verb phrase (verb and direct object).
(4) All activities are contained in the lowest-level decomposition.

ARROW RULES:
(1) Diagram boundary arrows must be plug-compatible.
(2) Each arrow has a unique label, which is a noun phrase (adjective and noun).
(3) Labels on arrow branches show flow restriction.
(4) Arrows are bundled to match activity level of detail.
(5) Arrows have rounded corners for ease of reading.

DIAGRAM RULES:
(1) Between three and six activities per diagram.
(2) ICOM codes define parent/child arrow connectivity.
(3) Diagrams show constraint; they are not data flow diagrams or flow charts.

MODEL RULES:
(1) A model is restricted to a single viewpoint and purpose.

Box Rules

Box Rule 1 states that only single-digit numbers should be used, and that they must appear in the lower-right corner of an activity box. Many IDEF0 authors have adopted the nonstandard convention of including the full node number in the lower-right corner of the box. Doing so violates the IDEF0 FIPS standard, and causes problems at the detail levels of the model, where the node number becomes quite long.

The IDEF0 reasoning for having a single-digit number in the lower-right corner of the box is that it uniquely identifies the activity box, since this number is appended to the diagram's node number to give the full, unique box identifier. Using a single digit has the advantage that, no matter how large the model grows, the length of the identifying number never interferes with the box name. Also, since the node number is visible at the bottom left of the diagram form, a reader can easily determine the full node number of the box if necessary. Note that although some IDEF0 computer support tools adopt other conventions for box numbers, the original type of single-digit box number should be used. Figure 6-1 illustrates both the original standard type and the nonstandard type of box number.

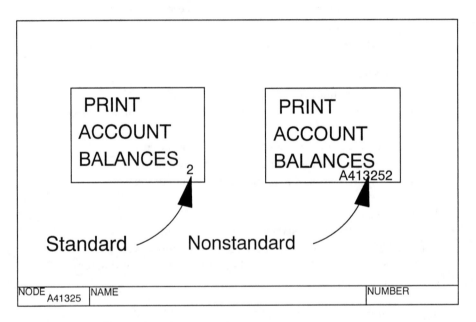

Figure 6-1: Box Numbering Convention.

Box Rule 2 states that each activity box must have at least one control and at least one output (it may or may not have any input). The rationale behind the control arrow requirement is that no activity can operate unless it has something controlling it. This rule requires the modeler to pause and consider what controls can be added to the diagram if all the initial data items are attributed but an uncontrolled activity is identified. Similarly, each activity also must have an output, or what is the point of doing the activity?

It may seem logical that the rule would require an input, as well as a control and an output. However, in some instances, an activity does not modify an existing entity; it creates an original, new entity. The input may be thought of as being created by the mechanism (person or system) that performs the activity. Figure 6-2 shows standard and nonstandard examples.

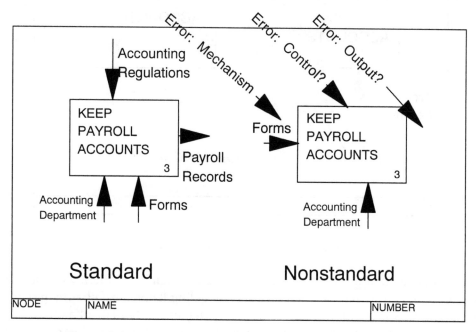

Figure 6-2: Input, Output, and Control Conventions.

The activity box KEEP PAYROLL ACCOUNTS on the left side of Figure 6-2 is syntactically correct. No input is necessary, but in this instance, some sort of payroll records should actually be included as an output to make the activity logically complete. However, adding Forms as an input, as shown on the right side of the figure, is incorrect, since Forms are merely a mechanism used to perform the activity.

Box Rule 3 states that an activity box must have an active verb phrase as its title, since the activity box represents an action, as defined by its decomposition. Quite often, an organization (an accounting department or manufacturing design department, for example) becomes so closely associated with a particular function or set of activities that the IDEF0 author may be tempted to use the organization name to label an IDEF0 activity box. This is nonstandard, as such a name reflects organization-based decomposition, not functional analysis. In the organization-based breakdown shown on the right side of Figure 6-3, a gerund is used, but IDEF0 requires that an active verb with its direct object modifiers (such as shown on the left side of the figure) be used in the correct naming process.

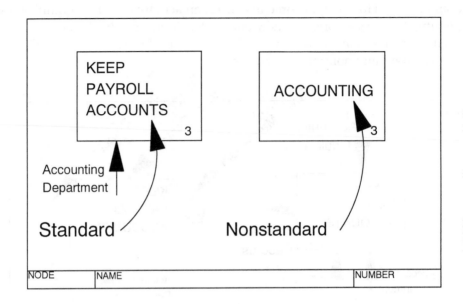

Figure 6-3: Activity Naming Convention.

Box Rule 4 states that all activity details must be contained at the lowest decomposed level. It is true that some hierarchical modeling languages other than IDEF0 include activities in the higher levels of the model, but in IDEF0, all activities are included in the most detailed child boxes in the model. The named parent box is just a placeholder for the decomposition—a hole into which may be plugged any activity diagram whose boundary arrows match (in structure and content) the arrows entering and leaving the parent box. The name helps communicate context to the reader but could logically be removed (leaving a blank box) without affecting the content of the model.

Arrow Rules

Arrow Rule 1 states that diagram boundary arrows must be plug-compatible. Of course, to be plug-compatible, the arrows entering and leaving a parent box must match (in structure and content) the boundary arrows of the decomposition (child) diagram. This is analogous to the concept of inserting electrical plugs into a receptacle: If the plug has three prongs, it will not fit into a receptacle having two holes. If there is a mismatch, then either some data has been omitted from the decomposition diagram or some data has mysteriously appeared in the decomposition without any record of its source or its destination in the parent diagram (see Figures 6-4 and 6-5, both of which depict the same model).

The IDEF0 modeling rule that all activity must be shown at the lowest level facilitates creation of a schematic, which displays the bottom-most diagrams on a large sheet of paper, with boundary arrows connecting the diagrams. The schematic enables study of the entire model or just a selected branch of the whole model. Since the decomposition of each activity is therefore a black box, individual diagrams or even entire model segments can be plugged into the model without causing unwanted side effects. Such "plug-compatible diagrams" represent alternative ways to perform the same activity, permitting what-if analysis of potential cost or of time savings, for example, when considering alternative TO-BE variations of specific processes (see Figure 6-4).

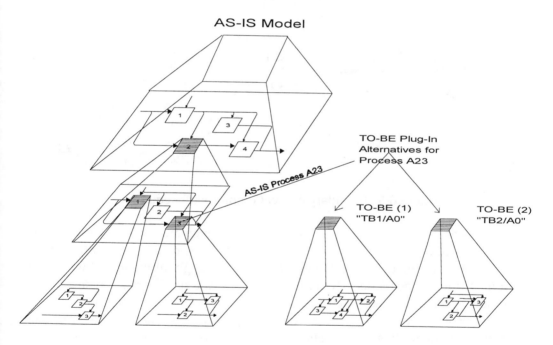

Figure 6-4: Plug-in Alternative TO-BE Processes.

Figure 6-5 shows that the parent box A23 (see Figure 6-4, for A23's position) has one input, one control, and one output. This matches the two alternative TO-BE processes and demonstrates there is plug compatibility. Of course, the author must check to ensure that the content of the three arrows is compatible and that the physical arrow structure matches. Some modelers break Arrow Rule 1 by showing a parenthesis at the unconnected end of the boundary arrow instead of an ICOM code (such as I1 for input 1 or C2 for control 2). This practice is dangerous, especially if it is used instead of a data arrow that is needed by an activity.

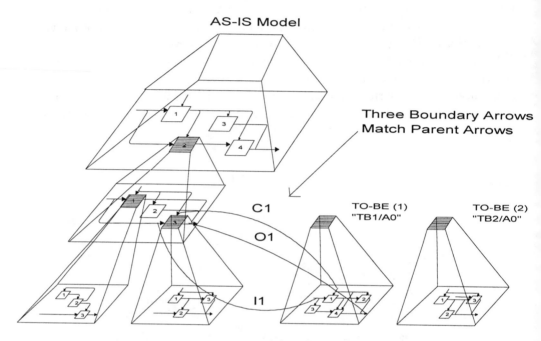

Figure 6-5: Boundary Arrow Compatibility Requirement.

Parentheses can be used with boundary arrows when any of the following three circumstances occurs. First, use parentheses when the data are only of interest at this level of detail, and when tracing the arrow throughout the model would add undue clutter to the model. Parentheses may indicate specific mechanisms for performing specific activities, such as know-how or education controls when these are the only controls on an activity. Second, use parentheses when the data represent an interface to another model, such as a model prepared from a different viewpoint. Third, use a parenthesis to indicate control or input data that may be included as a control or input on *all* activities in the decomposition.

In all cases, the modeler must include a note near the parenthesis indicating the source or target of the parenthetic data. This may be a DRE, indicating a location in an IDEF0 model (either the current model or a related model), or a statement "To All Activities," as in the third case described.

Arrow Rule 2 states that the label of each arrow must be unique. Logically, an arrow that is an input to an activity box cannot be the same arrow that is output from the box, since an input is modified by the activity to become an output. Typically, the author needs to add different adjectives to the output arrow labels, such as "revised" or "corrected," to indicate the change brought about by the activity. The uniqueness of each arrow label is important for proper arrow definition, but it is indispensable for building a database to support the system being modeled. Figure 6-6 illustrates incorrect and correct arrow labels.

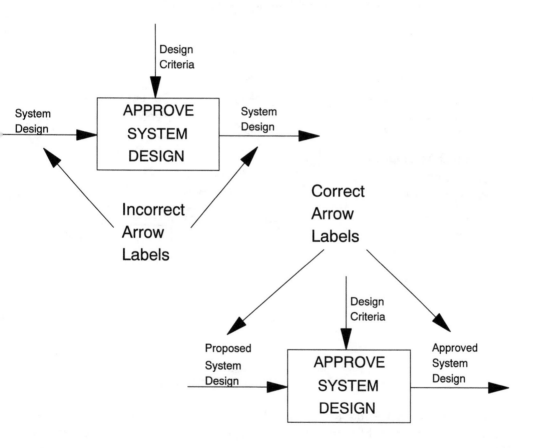

Figure 6-6: Arrow Uniqueness Rule.

Note that this second arrow rule does not state that each branch of every arrow must have a unique label displayed on the diagram; it merely says that the same name may not be used for two different arrows.

Arrow Rule 3 treats branch flow-restriction. Recall that, under the definition of arrows given in Chapter 4, a subbranch contains all of the content of the main branch, unless restricted by a label on the subbranch. For example, an arrow that splits into two branches does not indicate that the original content divides equally. Nor does it mean that all of the indicated content travels on one subbranch while none follows the other branch—unless a label appears on the other branch to restrict the flow. The reader must always assume the most general case in IDEF0— that all of the content flows to all of the branches—without attaching undocumented meaning to arrow branching and joining (see Figure 6-7).

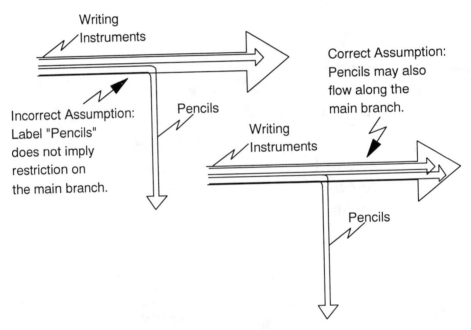

Figure 6-7: Arrow Flow-Restriction Rule.

Figure 6-8 illustrates *Arrow Rule 4* and shows how the use of rounded corners on arrows, rather than right-angle or square corners, improves the readability of an IDEF0 diagram.

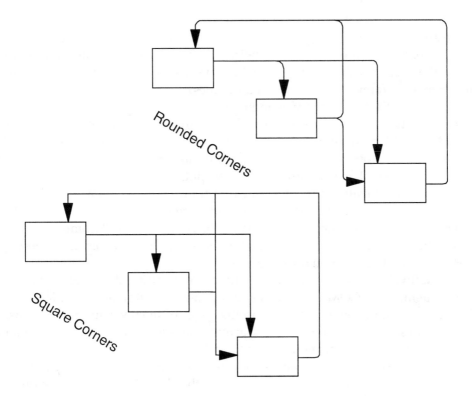

Figure 6-8: Arrow Corners.

Diagram Rules

Diagram Rule 1 states that there should be between three and six activities per diagram. Much has been made in this book of the fewer-than-six rule, making it clear that a modeler trying to handle more than six activities on a single diagram would encounter too much complexity to permit the type of communication power desired. However, little has been said of the three-or-greater part of the rule.

Diagram Rule 1 is based on the fact that IDEF0 is designed for functional analysis. If the author is modeling the logical functions of an enterprise, then specifying that at least three new activities are required in a decomposition results in a diagram that has a minimum amount of new detail. If a limit of only two activities were permitted, it would take the author considerably longer to reach the lowest level of detail. However, when the author is building an AS-IS model of an organization and the model is based on a familiar structural breakdown of activities, it is sometimes permissible to include a two-box activity diagram. This exception to Rule 1 is only applied when the natural enterprise structure has a two-way breakdown.

The argument for relaxing the method rule is that accomplishing the purpose of the model takes precedence over all else. That is, the model will communicate more to the user community if its structure matches a familiar, real-life structure rather than an unfamiliar model dictated by rules.

The three-activity minimum is intended for a model in which the author is exposing functional detail; it is not intended for an AS-IS picture that must be verified and for which consensus must be attained with the user community. An author may always obey the three-box rule, but this rigidity may lead to a less successful AS-IS model wherever natural two-way splits are encountered.

Diagram Rule 2 states that codes must be used to show connections between levels of decomposition. ICOM codes are off-page connectors used by IDEF0 to uniquely connect the arrow interfaces at the boundary of the decomposition diagrams. The arrow connectivity of an IDEF0 model cannot be verified unless the ICOM codes are displayed on the diagrams.

Most software tools have some convention for ensuring the parent/child connectivity using the ICOM code convention, such as automatically placing the ICOM codes from the parent box around the edges of the decomposition. Thus, if the author fails to connect the boundary arrows, he is left with ICOM code annotations around the edge of his new diagram, and the lack of connectivity is obvious to the reader. Any such diagram is logically incomplete, since the parent box shows all data items needed by the activity, but the child decomposition shows no use of one or more of those data items.

Diagram Rule 3 differentiates function-oriented IDEF0 diagrams from data flow or process-oriented diagrams. Individual IDEF0 activity boxes are intended to show multiple stimuli that produce one or more outputs whenever a prescribed set of inputs and controls are available. It is not necessarily true that for an activity to become active, all input and control arrows must contain data. Also, the content of the data included in an arrow may determine whether the activity activates, as well as whether outputs are produced.

This concept differs from that of a flow chart. In a flow chart, each box represents a unique activation. The flow chart defines the precise sequence of activations. In addition, the flow chart shows flow only, and does not depict the input, control, and output data shown in an IDEF0 diagram. Figure 6-9 illustrates the two types of diagrams.

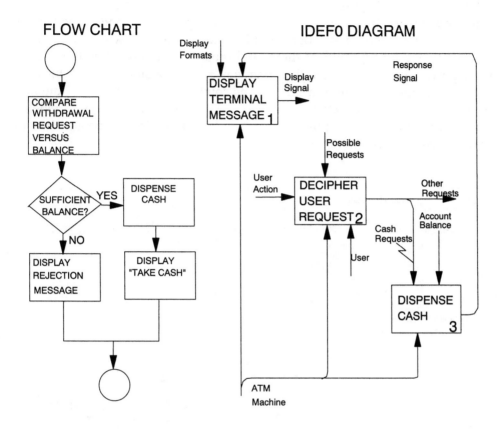

Figure 6-9: Flow Chart and IDEF0 Diagram Conventions Compared.

Model Rule

The only rule applied to the entire model is *Model Rule 1*—the requirement that the entire model have a single purpose and a single viewpoint. If there is a need for modeling a different viewpoint or purpose, a second model must be developed, and links between the two models must be included at points where they intersect.

The model's purpose is critical: The purpose must be clearly stated before modeling begins, or the modeling effort may become no more than an academic exercise. Bear in mind that the object of using IDEF0 is not to develop a model, but to create a baseline from which improvements can be defined. To ensure that a proper purpose is developed, modelers should open the purpose statement on the

A-0 diagram with the phrase: "The model will be used to . . ." By completing this statement with the objective to be achieved, and by examining each diagram as it is developed to see that it assists with the model's purpose, modelers will enhance the likelihood that the benefits of the IDEF0 modeling process will be achieved.

Likewise, the viewpoint of the model must be maintained as the subject is decomposed. By mixing more than one viewpoint in a single model, the author makes the model less communicative. The solution is to create a separate model for each viewpoint, connected via DRE or call arrows. The resultant models are much clearer, easier to manipulate, and easier to communicate to an audience than a single mixed-viewpoint model.

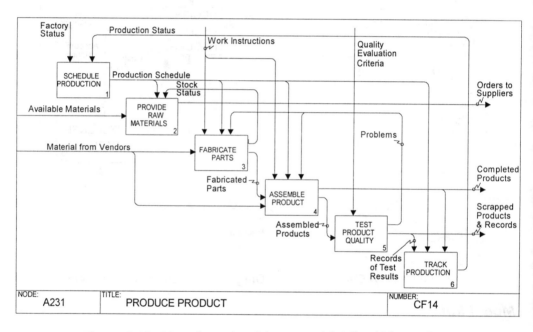

Figure 6-10: Manufacturing Diagram with Mixed Viewpoints.

Figure 6-10 presents a manufacturing enterprise model in which several viewpoints are mixed on a single diagram. The resultant complexity becomes more apparent when we consider the background and training of the various personnel who perform the activities shown on the model. Table 6-2 lists these personnel and illustrates a way of separating viewpoints. On the left side of the table, familiar titles of manufacturing process personnel are listed. Although a separate model could be produced corresponding to the viewpoint of each job classification, such an approach would be costly, time consuming, and would not result in the desired clarification of the model's complexity. Instead, a higher level of abstraction can be used to reduce the number of viewpoints required. That is, since personnel from a technical background typically can communicate with each other and have some knowledge of each other's work processes, it would seem reasonable to group the fabrication and assembly staffs into a single technical viewpoint.

Table 6-2.
Personnel, Their Activity Level, and Their Viewpoints.

TYPE OF PERSONNEL	ACTIVITY	VIEWPOINT
Shop Floor Manager	A1, A6	Management or Technical
Procurement Staff	A2	Financial
Machine Operators	A3	Technical
Assembly Personnel	A4	Technical
Quality Assurance Staff	A5	Quality

Taking this logic one step further, we can see that the shop floor manager must understand both the technical and the management viewpoints. However, he typically comes from a technical background and therefore probably fits best with the technical viewpoint model. The same logic might lead us to include the quality assurance staff in the technical viewpoint, but because so many quality initiatives are being pursued in today's environment, having a separate quality viewpoint is probably worthwhile.

This leaves the procurement personnel, who purchase the raw materials for fabrication and assembly. Their responsibilities, such as negotiations with vendors, stocking of parts, and processing of invoices and requisitions, represent a separate mindset from the other viewpoints; therefore, we would do well to record the financial viewpoint on a separate model.

Given the selected technical, quality, and financial viewpoints, the following diagrams show division of the original, mixed model into three separate models, with interconnecting arrows added as needed for communication. These diagrams illustrate how diverse viewpoints should be modeled separately, with links between the three models provided using DREs.

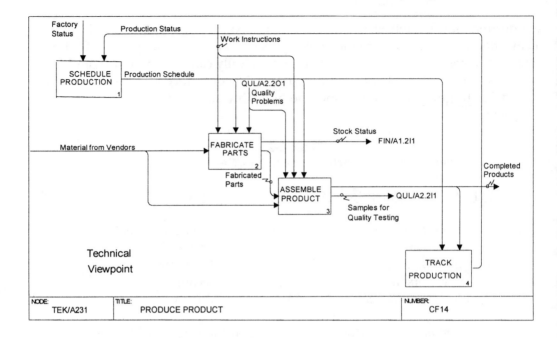

Figure 6-11: Manufacturing Diagram with Technical Viewpoint.

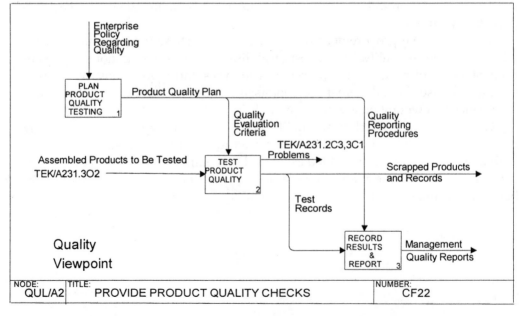

Figure 6-12: Manufacturing Diagram with Quality Viewpoint.

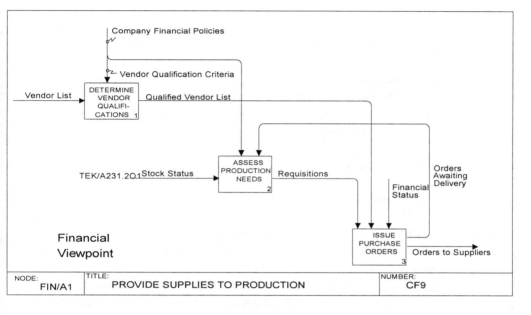

Figure 6-13: Manufacturing Diagram with Financial Viewpoint.

Looking at Figure 6-11, the technical viewpoint diagram, we see that box 3 (output 2) sends samples for quality testing to box 2 of the quality viewpoint diagram. In return, problems discovered by quality testing are sent to the technical viewpoint diagram via output 1 of box 2 of the quality model, and are received by the technical viewpoint diagram in control 3 to boxes 2 and 3 of the technical viewpoint diagram.

Similarly, the financial viewpoint model receives stock status via output 1 of box 2 of the technical viewpoint diagram. This is the only connection between the technical and financial viewpoint models, since the procurement people receive the stock status and issue purchase orders to obtain supplies when they run low (input 1 to box 2 and input 2 to box 3 of the technical viewpoint diagram).

In summary, the development of separate models for each viewpoint has the following advantages over development of a single model that mixes all viewpoints:

■ Focused diagrams are comparatively simple and easy to understand and can be tailored to specific cultures of people in an enterprise.

- Readers whose background corresponds to the model's focused view-point can understand the jargon and relate to details shown in the diagram.
- IDEF0 identifies interfaces between cultures (finance, management, quality assurance) as intersection arrows between the viewpoints; these intercultural interfaces typically represent key communication points, and they are often critical to any enterprise engineering effort.
- All viewpoints need not be decomposed to the same level of detail, thereby saving time, effort, and cost over decomposing a single model of all combined viewpoints.

Model Quality Measurement

In addition to hard and fast rules, a method also needs a defined set of quality criteria. That is, IDEF0 rules may be followed and the model produced may be standard IDEF0, but it may not be a good IDEF0 model. This section identifies standards for attaining quality in IDEF0 models and discusses how to avoid typical beginners' mistakes when using IDEF0 for the first time.

Quality Measurement Rule 1: Model Validation. The reader/author cycle review provides the best quality check of an IDEF0 model. It enables the author's peers to study the draft model and to formulate recommended improvements and corrections. It also provides a means of checking the communication power of the model, since if several readers have difficulty understanding a specific diagram, this tells the author that the diagram must be clarified before final release.

There have been instances when the reader/author cycle has broken down and the project manager has elected to abandon the method. The cause of the breakdown is typically the lack of response from the readers. The reader/author cycle is a critical aspect of IDEF0 modeling, and readers must support the process with a conviction that they can make real improvements through this approach.

An alternative quality-check approach is the walkthrough session conducted with a group of readers. This approach to model validation is less successful than the individual readership approach of the reader/author cycle, but it is a reasonable alternative to achieve validation and consensus.

The walkthrough approach generally is less satisfactory than a reader/author cycle because of the following reasons: The reader has less time to contemplate model details and recommended improvements; the walkthrough leader may foist his viewpoint on the audience by presenting the facts as he understands them, thereby undercutting the communication power of the model itself; and, lastly, vocal, persuasive members of the audience may be able to push their preferences, whereas more valid points may be overlooked due to emotional pressure. The level of acceptance of the model is marked in the kit cover sheet (upper right-hand corner) to clearly indicate model stability and acceptance. (Refer back to Figure 5-14 for a sample cover sheet.)

The basic measure of a model's quality is how it answers five general questions that support the purpose of the model and reveal the viewpoint covered by the model. These general-purpose model quality questions are

1. What controls each activity?
2. How does the activity respond to erroneous arrow content?
3. Is there any feedback to previously completed activities?
4. Which inputs and controls are used to produce each possible set of outputs?
5. Which events trigger activation of the diagram?

It is interesting to note that the last question treats the same concept as is currently becoming popular in the object-oriented methods community—the so-called use-case approach of Ivar Jacobson and others.[1]

Still, there needs to be a way of measuring model quality that is easier to apply than the general one of asking whether the model satisfies the purpose. The only such indicator to date is the ability of the model to address additional questions of purpose; as each diagram is completed and reviewed, quality can be further tested by developing other relevant, focused questions.

If the model is an AS-IS model of current operations, and the goal is to identify problem areas that need improvement, then questions regarding current operations are in order. Furthermore, if the goal is to develop remedies for these problems, then the level of detail of the model can be queried to determine whether sufficient information is present to design a solution. If it isn't, another decomposition layer or two is needed to provide additional detail. Some specific questions for checking quality in an AS-IS model are presented below.

1. Is there a single organization responsible for performing this activity? If not, further decomposition is needed.
2. Is there sufficient detail to determine operational cost, using activity-based costing? If not, further decomposition is needed.
3. What additional facts does this decomposition diagram provide?
4. Are the new facts related to the purpose? If they are not, try a different decomposition.
5. Are the new facts related to the viewpoint? If not, determine where a viewpoint shift occurred.

---

[1] I. Jacobson, et al. *Object-Oriented Software Engineering: A Use-Case Driven Approach* (Reading, Mass.: Addison-Wesley, 1992).

Quality Measurement Rule 2: Fog Factor Testing. The best test of the communication power of a diagram is the reaction received from the reader/author cycle critique. A second, more mechanical test of the readability of the model is provided by analyzing a diagram's cosmetic aspect: the layout, the number of arrows, and the arrow complexity, for example. This form of measuring diagram clutter tests the *fog factor.* Note that although the diagram may pass this test, it still may not be a high-quality diagram (that is, it may not present useful information, or it may use vague terminology on arrows and activities). However, if the diagram fails the fog factor test, it must be reworked if it is to fulfill its communication potential.

To calculate the fog factor, the modeler needs to answer a series of questions about a diagram. Each fog factor question has a numeric answer that is added to the prior sum to form a total fog factor. If this factor is greater than the maximum threshold, the diagram must be revised to reduce the factor. Each factor also has an individual maximum threshold, to prevent any one diagram element from being unreasonably complex. Fog factor questions and maximum threshold values are presented in Table 6-3.

Table 6-3.
Definition of the Fog Factor.

FACTOR	MAXIMUM THRESHOLD
F1. Number of boxes on the diagram	6
F2. Number of input arrows entering each box	3
F3. Number of control arrows entering each box	4
F4. Number of output arrows leaving each box	3
F5. Number of arrow forks or joins	(No Maximum)
F6. Number of arrow crossings	(No Maximum)

$$\text{Fog Factor} = F1 + F2 + \ldots + F6 \le 50$$

The fog factor formula adds the six basic sub-factors to produce a total value. If this value is above the suggested maximum, the diagram is too complex and needs to be reworked. A suggested maximum of fifty is used here, but a project may select its own maximum value, based on its readership.

Quality Measurement Rule 3: Arrow Label Precision. Box names and arrow labels are important to the diagram's message. Arrow labels are especially crucial, since the meaning of the box may be explored by studying its decomposition diagram but the meaning of the arrow is not so easily studied. (The reader would have to analyze the source and target of each arrow element to understand its complete meaning.) Furthermore, arrow labels give the reader early insight into what will occur in an activity box decomposition. Consider the arrow labels in the two treatments of MANUFACTURE PRODUCT in Figure 6-14. In the top example, the arrows show that user manuals are developed as part of the MANUFACTURE PRODUCT activity. In the bottom example, no such information is conveyed by the arrows. The box name could have been omitted in both cases, but the reader still could have inferred the name of the activity merely from the arrow labels.

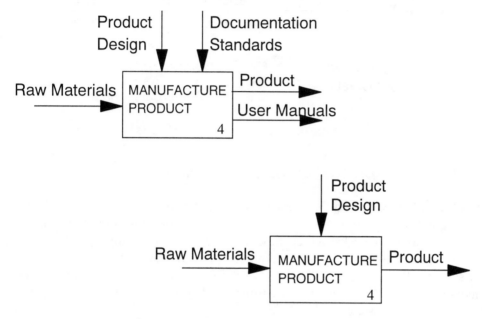

Figure 6-14: Comparison of Arrow Labels.

Clearly, the label an author chooses for each arrow is critical in conveying meaning to the reader. How specific the arrow labels are provides an important indication of how good the model is. Two measures for judging the quality of box names and arrow labels can be derived from comparisons of function versus form and of explicitness versus vagueness. Figure 6-15 illustrates how varied names and labels might be used for the same box and arrows.

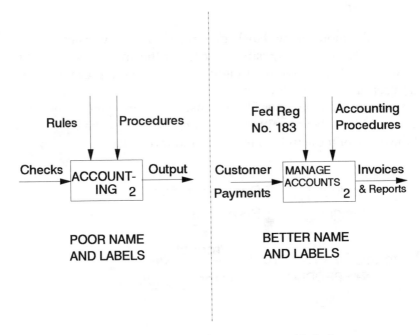

Figure 6-15: Comparing Names and Labels.

The labels on the arrows and the name of the box shown on the left side of the figure are vague and imprecise, chosen to focus on the form rather than the function. Arrow 2I1 is labeled Checks, which describes the form of the input, not its function. The input could just as easily have been provided by cash, wire transfer, or one of several other alternative forms. On the right side of the figure, the arrow 2I1 labeled Customer Payments is more functionally oriented and is not dependent on the form of transmission.

The box name on the left side of the figure is similarly form-oriented rather than functional. Also, it is not composed of a verb-and-noun phrase—as is standard for IDEF0—it is a gerund, a form of activity name that comes from organizational thinking. The use of this sort of nonstandard box name by an IDEF0 author invariably means that he is thinking about the department rather than about what the department does—again, form instead of function; since a person from a different company's accounting department might perform different activities, a better choice for the box name is MANAGE ACCOUNTS, as shown on the right-hand side of the figure.

The remaining arrow labels in the example at the left side of Figure 6-15 further illustrate names that lack precision: Not all company rules and procedures control box 2. Arrow labels should enable the reader to understand precisely what information is used by the activity, as is communicated in the diagram on the right. Similarly, the vague output label on 2O1 is vastly improved by the label Invoices & Reports.

Quality Measurement Rule 4: Simplistic Diagram Story. Sometimes, a kit of diagrams from an author may seem too simple. There may be almost no arrows, and few, if any, feedback arrow paths. To determine whether the kit of diagrams is, in fact, too simple, the author must evaluate his kit of diagrams by answering key questions and by submitting it to walkthroughs in which an audience of experts tests it in the context of typical situations and events. The author must explain the way his kit of diagrams handles each situation. For example, imagine a model for the activity of reviewing bids for new business. In Figure 6-16, the activity is decomposed into five sub-activities. At first glance, the diagram appears to represent a thorough breakdown of the process, and the story is easy to understand.

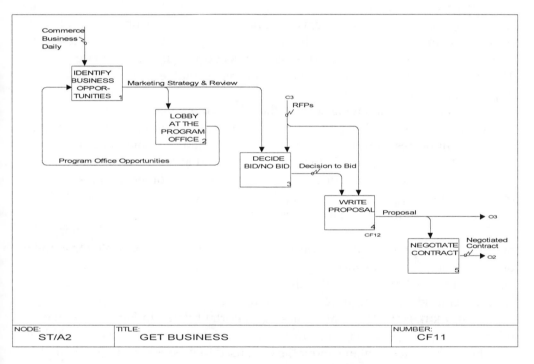

Figure 6-16: A Too-Simple Diagram.

Box 1, IDENTIFY BUSINESS OPPORTUNITIES, is controlled by the CBD (*Commerce Business Daily*), which announces government business opportunities. Using this control, opportunities are pursued and passed along to lobbyists as part of the marketing strategy. Box 2, LOBBY AT THE PROGRAM OFFICE, uses this control to determine where there is a real opportunity. Based on the Program Office Opportunities feedback, specific opportunities are selected and used in the bid/no bid decision in box 3. If the decision is to bid, a proposal-writing effort is triggered, and the government's request for proposal (RFP) is used as a control on the proposal content and schedule. Finally, the proposal is submitted, and the contract is negotiated.

The story this diagram tells is correct, but it is not complete. Recall that part of the job of the author is to examine each box and to ask key questions, such as: Is this all that controls this activity? What happens if one or more of the arrows is incorrect? Are there additional outputs that may be produced by this activity? Is there any feedback to other activities? Recall as well that the quality of the diagram depends on its ability to answer questions related to the purpose of the model.

Applying these questions to the diagram in Figure 6-16 results in the addition of several arrows to make the diagram more complete and useful, as shown in the revised Figure 6-17. For example, is the CBD the only control on the identification of business opportunities? No, the enterprise's plans and charters determine which opportunities are in their strategic plans and which should not be pursued. Therefore, box 1 needs an additional control (plans, budgets, charters) to take this important factor into account.

The results of the lobbying activity (box 2) are more than just a list of opportunities to be considered. The lobbyists get to know the personnel at the government procurement offices, and therefore gain very important information to pass along to the bid/no bid decision. If the customer feels that the enterprise has a good company image, this is important to know. If the customer favors a different enterprise, and the process of bidding the RFP is a waste of time in the opinion of the lobbyists, then this is also important to know.

Box 3, DECIDE BID/NO BID, in Figure 6-16 shows the results of the decision to bid but not what happens when the decision is not to bid. The rationale for a no-bid decision is important feedback information for future use by the enterprise management and the lobbyists (maybe they can improve the company image or otherwise mitigate a factor that caused the no-bid decision).

Box 4, WRITE PROPOSAL, is also missing important data. In Figure 6-16, there is no input to the proposal-writing effort, and the controls are the decision to bid and the RFPs only. After thinking about the data used in proposal writing, the modeler probably should conclude that copies of old proposals are essential for generation of good new proposals. Also, the strategic planning that took place in box 1 should have a key controlling role in the content and presentation form of the proposal. Therefore, the marketing strategy from box 1 should be used as a control to box 4, as well as to boxes 2 and 3. Also, a key element in proposal preparation is the ability to get temporary support for the proposal-writing effort from key personnel in widespread areas of the enterprise organization. Therefore, the call for needed support is added to the proposal-writing process of box 4.

Although Figure 6-17 shows the results of examining the activities, asking key questions, and running what-if scenarios, the model is still not absolutely complete. However, it is now ready for reader review and comment in the reader/author cycle.

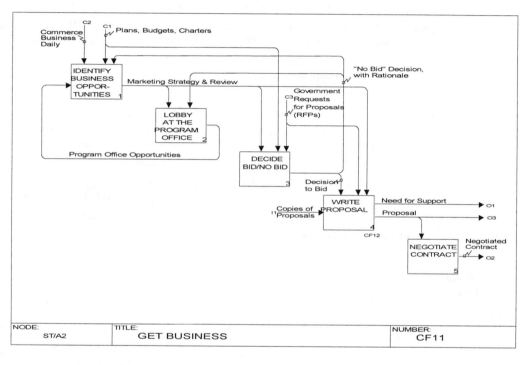

Figure 6-17: Revised Diagram.

Quality Measurement Rule 5: Arrow Bundle Grouping. The most common problem new authors demonstrate is the tendency to create arrows for individual pieces of data, rather than for bundles of data, or conduits. This leads to diagrams with so many arrows that the message is obscured; reading the diagram becomes an exercise in following train tracks rather than in concentrating on the message. Arrows are really conduits that contain other arrows, similar to an electrical conduit, as we saw in Figure 5-11. By gathering individual arrows into bundles, that is, into groups of similar arrows, the author reduces the complexity of the arrow pathways on the diagram, thereby making the arrow level of detail match that of the activity boxes with which the arrows interface.

The problem new authors have matching data arrow levels with activities stems from the fact that most people are proficient at grouping activities, such as in organization structures, but they are not accustomed to grouping data. Paradoxically, everyone from the president down to the individual contributors in an enterprise is used to dealing with individual pieces of data and individual documents, but the grouping of data entities into bundles and the naming of these combined arrow conduits are not familiar activities.

Arrows tend to branch and uncover detailed data interfaces as the activity diagram decomposition progresses. This permits the story to unfold without railroad-track arrow patterns that are difficult to follow and that may distract non-technical staff.

Figures 6-18 and 6-19 illustrate, respectively, the incorrect and correct use of arrow bundling. In the railroad-track version, each piece of data used by the strike leader is shown on an arrow. In the second diagram, the pieces of data have been bundled into two arrows instead of five, with four pieces of data (mission concept, mission objective, rules of engagement, and strike leader's checklist) bundled into a single arrow labeled Guidance Documents. As the activities on the diagram are decomposed, four individual pieces of data will split out as arrow branches and will be shown being used by specific sub-activities. The level of detail of the arrows should match the level of detail of the boxes if the diagram is going to communicate effectively to an audience.

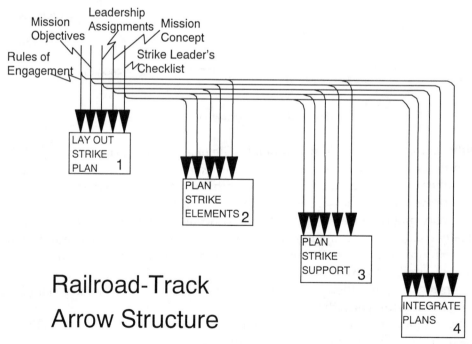

Railroad-Track Arrow Structure

Figure 6-18: Lack of Arrow Bundling.

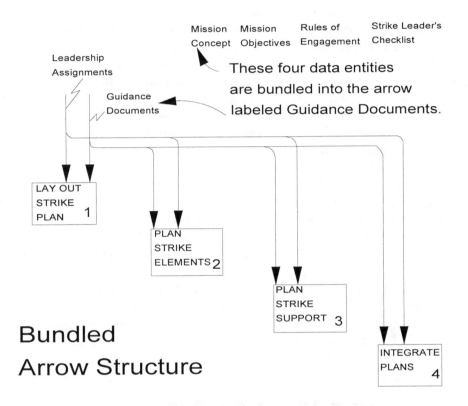

Figure 6-19: Equivalent Diagram with Arrow Bundling.

Quality Measurement Rule 6: Descriptive Arrow Labels. Everyone is familiar with the physical form by which information is conveyed (in a printed form or on a computer screen, for example), but what is most important in an IDEF0 model is the information being conveyed, not the form itself. For example, the output from any computer program might be on a computer screen or printout, but data labeled "computer screen output" is not helpful for IDEF0 communication or for conveying an understanding of the modeled process. A much better label would be "project budget" or "monthly expenses," or words to describe the functional content of the arrow. A good rule to follow is, avoid using generic nouns such as "input," "output," "report," or "document" in the label of an arrow on an IDEF0 diagram.

Quality Measurement Rule 7: Precise Control Arrow Content. As IDEF0 authors decompose activities and create ever-more detailed diagrams, they often do not pay sufficient attention to control arrow content. Control arrows must split into finer, more specific content to match the level of generality of the activity boxes. For example, a common mistake is to carry the product design or the company standards as a control to all boxes as they are decomposed. Instead, the author should question what portion of the design or standard is actually needed by the activity at hand, and then he should branch the control arrow, labeling the branch with the precise portion of the main arrow that is needed. For example, a BILL THE CUSTOMER activity need only use the company's billing-standard procedure, not the entire set of company standards.

Quality Measurement Rule 8: Correct Identification of Controls. One of the decisions most frequently faced by IDEF0 authors is determining, "Is this a control or an input?" This question stems from the common practice of allowing only one form of entity to enter into an activity, and from not splitting out the controlling entities from the inputs. Another cause of confusion is the fact that, at the higher (more general) levels of an IDEF0 model, the conduits of bundled arrows contain individual internal arrows, some of which will act as inputs while others will act as controls after decomposition. The general rule is: If the arrow has a controlling influence on the activity, then consider it a control until its contents break down into individual input and control arrows at the model's detailed levels. In general, if the arrow label contains any of the control-oriented nouns listed in Table 6-4, then it should be considered a control.

Table 6-4.
Common Labels for Control-Oriented Arrows.

CONTROL	INPUT
Requirement	Raw Material
Standard	Product
Policy	Part or Kit
Directive	Blank Form

Without a clear understanding of control in IDEF0, the author cannot be certain whether a specific arrow should be shown as an input or as a control. In some cases, the confusion is whether an arrow is a control or a mechanism. Authors experienced in other modeling methods are usually no help in this debate, since other methods do not distinguish between inputs and controls, and often do not show the mechanism at all. To further confuse the issue, other methods have a different meaning for the concept of control (see the discussion of business rules as used by the DoD, below).

Some IDEF0 authors argue that all arrows are controls, since the content of the arrow "controls how the activity works." This is true, but it is also loose thinking and not helpful for BPR purposes. The argument here confuses the term "control" with "constraint."

Precision in defining the role of an arrow is important for BPR purposes, since the author may wish to propose several different mechanisms (for example, an automated approach and a manual approach). Similarly, he may wish to examine the rate at which input is processed or how management controls may be applied to the operation of the process.

In the FIPS definition, the rule for input arrows states that "the input is modified by the activity to produce the output." In general, this is a good rule to use, since it is simple to understand and apply, and it works in the majority of cases. However, this rule is sometimes inconclusive and a more precise rule must be invoked.

The method of making a distinction is to ask *the purpose served by the arrow* as it relates to the activity shown on the IDEF0 diagram, that is, its *role* in the process. If its role is to be acted upon by the activity, then it is an input. If its role is to control how the activity works, then it is a control. If its role is to perform the activity, then it is a mechanism.

The concept of business rules, as employed by the DoD, represents a different kind of control. Constraints, in the form of business rules, are derived from interviews with office personnel, and interview details indicate relationships between objects in the model. For example, the statement "we build three types of airplanes: crop dusters, fighter planes, and small private jets" defines the products produced by an enterprise, and therefore the statement describes what controls (constrains) the enterprise. The complete set of business rules is known as the control architecture of the enterprise.

However, this is not what is meant by "control" in IDEF0, where control describes how an activity performs its function. For example, a steering wheel controls the direction of the vehicle, and the lock controls access to the vehicle. The primary purpose is to control the activity.

For the DoD, business rules define the infrastructure of the enterprise's objects. Therefore, the control architecture specified by the business rules provides important information in identifying details of the enterprise, the meaning of its terminology, and the impact of proposed changes on these objects. IDEF0 controls, on the other hand, define how to manage the operation of the enterprise's processes— which objects and artifacts have what effect on which other processes, including side effects and subsequent cost and schedule impacts. Clearly, both types of information are important in implementing a BPR effort.

Quality Measurement Rule 9: Viewpoint Focus. If the diagrams seem to show many kinds of data from different viewpoints of a system, the modeler should check back to see what viewpoint statement is provided on the A-0 diagram. If none is provided, it is probable that the author did not understand the viewpoint concept. Mixed viewpoint diagrams are hard to read and understand, and they should be remodeled.

Quality Measurement Rule 10: Text Selection. The text that accompanies a diagram should be generated after the model has reached at least the Recommended level of approval. If the text is written too soon, information may be included in the text that properly belongs in the model itself. Typically, the text will have to be rewritten repeatedly as the diagrams are modified during the reader/author cycle. A common mistake with text is to describe each of the boxes in the diagram. Such detail is more properly shown by way of the child diagrams and should not be included in the parent text. The purpose of the text is to highlight key features, not to explain the breakdown of the boxes.

Quality Measurement Rule 11: Function and Design Separation. A primary goal in good system development is to keep the functional model separate from the design model. That is why *what* the system must do is quite separate from *how* a solution is designed to do it. Often there are several designs to match a single functional view before the final, best solution can be completed. To help a modeler separate function from design, a commenter might ask whether the details describe what must be done or just one method of designing a function. For example, a message may be sent to a manager, but this can be accomplished by telephone, fax, radio, carrier pigeon, and so on. The fact that the message must be conveyed and what information is in the message have to do with function; the form in which it is conveyed is a design detail.

Table 6-5 summarizes common errors made by authors, including a recommended remedy for each type of error.

Table 6-5.
Common Mistakes and Their Solutions.

MISTAKE	SOLUTION
Simplistic Diagrams	Walkthroughs
Pieces of Data on General-Level Activities	Bundling
Wrong Form of Breakdown	Data List
Sequence Instead of Constraint	Function, Not Time
Control Arrows Lack Precision	Labels on Branches
Arrow Labels Show Form Not Constraint	Purpose of Arrow Content
Control versus Input Controversy	Data List Step
Trivial Usage for Documentation	A-0 Statement
Concept of Viewpoint and Its Use	A-0 Statement
Understanding of Mechanisms and Calls	Support Levels
Arrow Forks and Joins	Branch Label Constraint
Use of Text	Highlights, Not Description
Design versus Function Models	What versus How Separation

Achieving Model Quality

Given the same topic and the same source documents and/or interviews with experts, each person in a roomful of people will come up with a different first diagram. Some diagrams will be better than others. That is, one diagram will be easier to understand, will convey a more meaningful message to the intended audience, and will fulfill the model's purpose better than other versions of the diagram. A friend of mine calls the inferior diagrams "content free."

What makes this difference? and, What can an IDEF0 manager of a modeling project do to guard against spending excessive amounts of time and money only to wind up with a content-free model? The critical difference comes from the author's selection of the three-six activity breakdown when developing a new diagram.

Through this book's discussion of arrow labels, we have seen that the careful selection of labels to depict the content of the arrows is essential to creating superior models. But the decomposition itself is the nucleus of the message conveyed by the diagram, since it provides the baseline for communicating information about the topic. If the decomposition is not carefully chosen, the labels on the arrows cannot make the model helpful, no matter how well they are selected.

Recommendation 1: Model for the Purpose. Recall that the primary means of judging model quality is by assessing whether it successfully answers questions relative to the model's purpose. In other words, if the model's purpose is to improve work flow, does the model highlight work-flow problems? If the model's purpose is to provide a functional requirements definition for a user interface to a new computer system, does the model break down the functions into manual versus automated functions supported by the computer? If the model's purpose is to define the roles and responsibilities of the present staff and organization, does the model break down the activities so that a specific department in the organization is identified with each of the activity boxes in the model?

The answer to the above questions should be yes, if the model is capable of fulfilling its purpose and is of high quality. If the model breakdown shows activities and interfaces that are not helpful in accomplishing the purpose of the modeling effort, then the diagrams will be judged "content free."

The key is to focus on the model's purpose, and then to cluster the activities into objective-oriented activities, adding appropriate arrow labels to provide a meaningful diagram. Figures 6-20 and 6-21 illustrate the concept.

Let me give a real-world example of modeling the purpose. As I described briefly in Chapter 5, the project I was involved in was one whose purpose was to identify immediate improvements in the current operation and to lay the groundwork for more major reorganization and downsizing. The merging of two different facilities had already taken place (by brute force), and the strategy of the AS-IS modeling effort was to highlight problem areas resulting from the already implemented merger.

The subject of the model was the merging of VA and military hospitals by the DoD. As was stated in Chapter 5, one function of the admissions office was to enter patient data into a patient admissions database, which would then track the patient through his stay at the hospital. The first attempt to develop a diagram of this process showed personnel gathering data from the admissions forms, entering this into the computer, comparing existing records for any prior patient history, and producing various reports once the correctness of the information had been verified. This breakdown makes a nice, informative diagram, as shown in Figure 6-20.

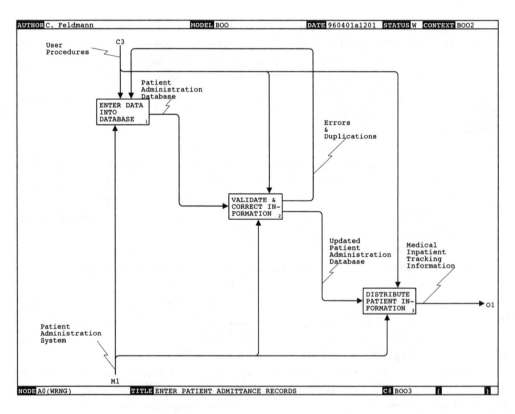

Figure 6-20: Content-Free Diagram.

However, the purpose of the effort was to highlight problem areas, and the modeling of the data-entry activity as described herein does not focus on this purpose. The actual operations staff of the data-entry office had a serious problem: The two merged organizations had different computer systems, and data had to be copied out of one computer system and entered into the other if both partners in the merger were to have access to needed information. Furthermore, one or the other of the two databases was often missing patient information or had incorrect information, causing severe problems later on. Figure 6-21 shows the same model as in the previous diagram, but this time with a focus on the operational problems, not on the basic function being performed.

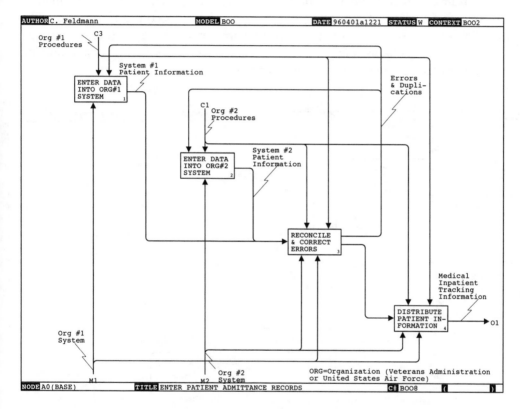

Figure 6-21: Clarified Diagram.

For anyone examining this diagram, the non-value-added nature of the duplicate entry and cross-checking effort was obvious, without the modeler even getting into concerns about incomplete or erroneous information. Examination of the diagram resulted in a reengineering recommendation to create an automated link through a single data-entry package, and then, at a later date, to create a single, totally merged VA/DoD patient administration computer system.

Recommendation 2: Focus on Function. Let's look at a second example, also from my consulting experience, that illustrates the common mistake of focusing too much on the form of the information rather than its function. A modeling project at the Department of Energy was intended to develop a revised accounting process. The existing process was unevenly applied, with the Chicago office's eight staff members monitoring more than $4 billion worth of contracts. Some contracts were very loosely scrutinized, while others were overanalyzed (accounting for every last pencil, eraser, paper clip, staple, and so on). A TO-BE model was to be developed that showed a process of reasonably careful audits that could be applied to all projects in a standard way.

In order to develop the AS-IS model, the staff was trained in the IDEF0 method and assigned the job of modeling the office's existing accounting process. This modeling effort resulted in diagrams similar in appearance to Figure 6-22, which focuses on the mechanism and the form of the data (reports, input data, and the like) rather than on the purpose of the data.

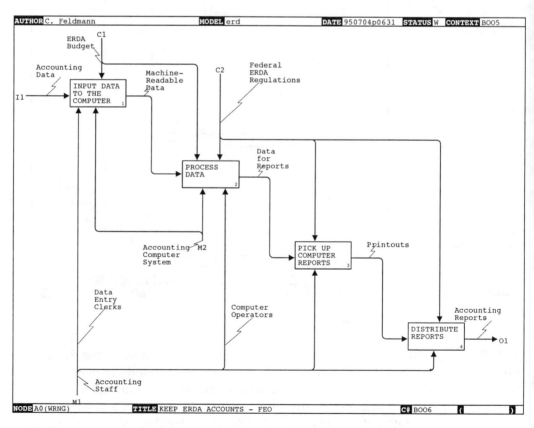

Figure 6-22: First Attempt at an ERDA Diagram.

To redirect their modeling effort away from mechanisms and toward purpose, we used the following set of function-oriented questions that would draw out more helpful information:

What kinds of data are input?
What does the computer do with the input data?
What data are in the reports that are printed and distributed?
What are the reports used for?

This interview format provided the right approach, but without persistent questioning, it didn't always help to dig out the kind of content that was needed. For example, when asking the second question (What does the computer do with the input data?), I expected an answer such as, "The computer calculates the taxes and salary and produces the payroll." I was disappointed to get a general response, "The computer processes the data."

Too-general answers were rejected, and additional question-and-answer sessions were held until the functional perspective was finally achieved, and we were able to produce an informative diagram, similar to that shown in Figure 6-23.

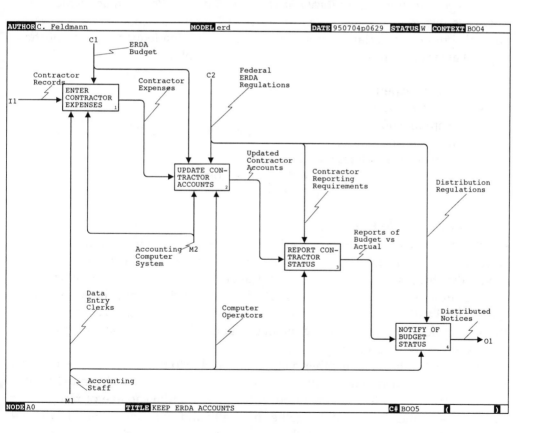

Figure 6-23: Function-Oriented Improved Diagram.

Why is this diagram better than the first? It is superior because it provides a baseline from which to accomplish the purpose of the model: to identify and define standard contractor controls. For example, the specific contractor records, reporting requirements, and distribution regulations could be defined overall, and then the process could be followed by all ERDA contract monitors to develop and implement an evenly applied contract-tracking process.

Management Lessons Learned

Instead of depending on the technically oriented model quality factors described above, the success or failure of an IDEF0 business process reengineering effort often depends on several key management issues. The problems and solutions described in the following sections should enable managers of IDEF0 reengineering projects to achieve greater success.

Management Rule 1: Encourage Model Project Support. Proper management support is as important to the success of an IDEF0 project as good technical results. Several types of essential support are listed below. Inadequacy in any of these support areas could result in significant project disruption.

- trained, experienced author staff
- trained readers and commenters
- computer support tools
- kit-processing support
- interview time allocation
- responsive, carefully selected technical committee
- management visibility and interest

The first two support factors deal with personnel. As with any endeavor, the staff selected to work on the project is critical to its success. IDEF0 authors must be selected with great care to maximize the chances of success in generating a useful model that fulfills its purpose. A technical staff member who is knowledgeable only about an extremely narrow aspect of the enterprise is not likely to make a good IDEF0 author. However, such a person usually makes an excellent reader in the R/A cycle, since he will probe the fine detail and not permit the diagram to be approved if it contains errors.

An IDEF0 author, on the other hand, must be able to think top-down, since this hierarchical approach matches the structure of an IDEF0 model. He must be able to think about subjects at a general level of detail, and be capable of recognizing groups of activities that cluster together naturally and share a common functional bond. At the same time, a good IDEF0 author must be able to analyze and synthesize a large number of facts and disjointed pieces of information. People who can see commonality between activities and things that seem unrelated to most other people are well suited for analyzing an AS-IS model and for proposing reengineering changes that will save time and cost through shared resources and support systems.

Perhaps the most serious emotional threat to the support of an IDEF0 business process reengineering project is the concern that the IDEF0 model will result in a loss of jobs. Any time business processes are examined with an eye toward optimization and cost reduction, people fear job loss. The best way to handle this fear is through solid management support. If management is convinced that the IDEF0 model will result in a more efficient and cost-effective operation, then it will support the project when objections come from the staff. Of course, each manager must be confident that the model being developed is accurate and complete and that planned changes are realistic. By indicating that the goal is a positive one, such as expanded capacity rather than staff reduction, managers can further minimize fears.

Management Rule 2: Reduce Model Development Cost. Creating IDEF0 models can be expensive and time-consuming. This section lists factors to monitor and presents techniques for reducing the cost of model development. Some key factors are

- experienced head IDEF0 author
- well-defined model purpose and viewpoint
- efficient operation of the reader/author cycle
- rapid definition of the top level of the model
- reusable models
- proficient knowledge of decomposition and abstraction

The skill of the head author is critical to cost-effective IDEF0 modeling. All items on the list above are related to the experience and know-how of the head author, but a major obstacle to hiring the most experienced candidate is that well-done IDEF0 models look deceptively simple. Conclusions such as "I can do that myself. We don't need to hire an expensive analyst!" may lead a client to base a hiring decision on the analyst's charge per day, not on his IDEF0 experience. An experienced IDEF0 author can usually produce three or four times the number of diagrams per day as an inexperienced author, and the quality and utility of these diagrams are remarkably superior. The IDEF0 modeling field needs a value-per-dollar criterion rather than a dollar-per-hour criterion to select the most cost-effective analyst for the job.

One excellent way to control the cost of model development, then, is to select a head author with a track record of successful IDEF0 application. An author's experience can especially affect startup costs, and reuse of previous models can contribute to further savings.

During one of my first model development projects, measurements were made of the effort required in building models. The statistics showed a basic rule: The time to develop a diagram at a given level of the model is equal to the square of the time to develop the next lower level. Thus, if it took sixteen days to develop A0, it should take four days to develop A1, two days to develop A11, and so forth.

This is an interesting statistic, rooted in the fact that the top level of the model involves mentally laying out the entire system to ensure that the scope of the subject is encompassed. A large list of data elements must be defined and clustered into the arrow pipelines, and the activities must be grouped into six or fewer major general activities. Once the top level is completed, the author uses those data lists and activity subgroupings to start the next decomposition. As each new lower level is decomposed, the detail becomes more bounded and easier to grasp.

Of course, working against this increase in productivity is the decrease caused by the addition of new authors as the decomposition progresses. At the top level, one author is laying out the entire system. At the next level, several authors may take over, each one decomposing a box on the A0 diagram. These new authors must become familiar with the model's breakdown and discover what was in the mind of the head author when he developed the A0 diagram.

Since development of the top few layers of the model is so costly and time-consuming, it seems logical that having a library of existing model tops would be of great benefit at project start-up time. Although beneficial in many cases, having a library of model tops can be a negative factor, since the chief author must be free to use his creativity and think for himself; he must not feel obliged to shoehorn his new model structure into one that does not really fit the system he is modeling.

However, experience suggests that there is great similarity between the models in a given topic area. The ICAM model of aerospace manufacturing showed that there was far more similarity between the major aerospace companies' activities than any of the companies were willing to admit at the outset of the program. The same is true in business process reengineering, whether at the various military facilities or in the financial offices of large corporations. Therefore, the development and reuse of a topically organized model library is quite feasible.

The use of such a library provides other benefits, too: insurance against overlooking a piece of the system; common terminology, using a central, well-defined glossary; high-level bundling of arrows into large pipes; reasonable naming and labeling at the start; and general, prior acceptance of the model. With reuse, the avoidance of common authoring problems augments the communication power of the IDEF0 model at the beginning of a new project, and increases understanding and acceptance of the model.

Another major cause of wasted time and of low-utility modeling is not knowing when to stop a decomposition sequence or when to switch to a different viewpoint or level of abstraction. The basic question that should be asked at each new level of decomposition is, "Is there further detail needed to satisfy the purpose from this viewpoint?" It is much easier, especially at the lower levels of a model, to continue the decomposition once a group of authors gets rolling than to consider whether it would be more cost-effective and beneficial to switch to a different viewpoint or level of abstraction.

There are four main reasons why a decomposition sequence should be stopped: First, an activity may be decomposed elsewhere in the model. Second, the author may wish to plug in alternative decompositions at a particular node. Third, a drop in level of abstraction may be needed to expose essential detail. The fourth reason is that no further detail may be needed from a particular viewpoint. If any of these circumstances are present, the IDEF0 project itself may be in trouble and should be reevaluated.

```
┌─────────────┐
│             │
│  APPENDICES │────────────────────────────────────────▶
│             │
└─────────────┘
```

The following five Appendices contain previously published papers, models, and other background information that illustrate issues relevant to IDEF0 and the tools and techniques discussed in the text.

Types of Models and Forms of Breakdown

No mention has been made thus far of *types of models* or *forms of breakdown* that a modeler may employ when analyzing a topic top-down. That is because an analyst can develop IDEF0 models without being aware of this distinction. He can still use IDEF0 effectively by keeping his purpose for developing the model clearly before him. But in this Appendix, we go deeper into using model types and breakdown forms to become even more effective in modeling the purpose and in communicating with the intended audience.

Modeling the Function versus the Process

In IDEF0, either the *functions* or the *processes* of an enterprise may be modeled. A function-oriented model defines the *types* of activities that are performed irrespective of time; a process-oriented model shows *sequences* of activities performed by the enterprise. For example, a function model contains a single activity box for each type of activity (design, manufacturing, management, and so forth), whereas a process model contains multiple activity boxes of the same type—one for each time a function is performed. Figure A-1 illustrates the concept with an example from a manufacturing enterprise.

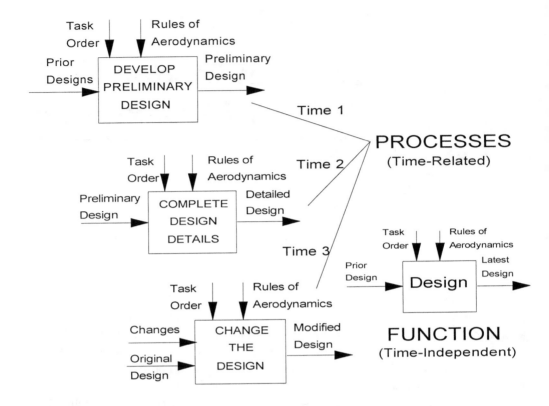

Figure A-1: Process versus Function Modeling.

The diagram in Figure A-1 is not intended to represent a single IDEF0 diagram; it shows individual activity boxes from several diagrams to illustrate the differences.

On the left side of the figure, three separate processes are drawn for the design function based on when the function is used: a preliminary design, a detailed design, and a design change process. On the lower right side of the figure, a single box in a function model depicts the design function regardless of when it occurs— in other words, what it means to do design in general. From this example, we see that a process-type model is by nature much larger than a function model, since each activity box must be repeated each time it occurs during the enterprise's daily operation.

Aside from being much larger than the function model, the process model scatters each function over a widespread location in the model structure, and this makes it more difficult for the viewer or analyst to envision commonalities to exploit when reengineering the enterprise. In an IDEF0 function model, all of the design activities are modeled in one place, and all of the required functionality is analyzed cohesively. For example, an effect of the process model is to increase the likelihood of defining several computer packages to assist a designer—one for each process—whereas the function model would yield a single-computer support system for all uses of a function (a common design system, for example).

On the negative side, it is much harder for the staff of an enterprise to check the correctness and completeness of a function model than of a process model. This is because each staff member may envision himself performing his daily activities in the process model ("I do this, then I do this. . . ."), rather than imagining how others do similar tasks and synthesizing all usages into a single function.

An analyst may use this phenomenon to his advantage by creating a process model first, checking the facts with staff, and then developing a function model later, after identifying the common functions scattered around the process model and grouping them by commonality of function. Process improvements may then be designed to serve a wide variety of related processes, based upon the gathering of all uses of the function by the enterprise.

Forms of Activity Breakdown

Either form of model—function or process—may use one of several methods for modeling activities in finer detail. For purposes of this Appendix, we examine the four most common forms of breakdown: decomposition, sequential, organizational, and split-by-type (SBT), so that an analyst may choose which form best suits his purpose. In the following paragraphs, I define each form of breakdown and use a repeating example to illustrate the way each form of breakdown approaches the same subject.

The original form of breakdown used by SADT is *decomposition,* in which the parent activity decomposes into its sub-activities. Figure A-2 shows that the function "Report to Management" includes a status-gathering function, a documentation function, and a presentation function. These three functions are different in nature from one another; they require different skills and different detailed activities. A staff member who gathers prescribed data may not be good at writing. A staff member who writes well may not be as effective when making presentations to management.

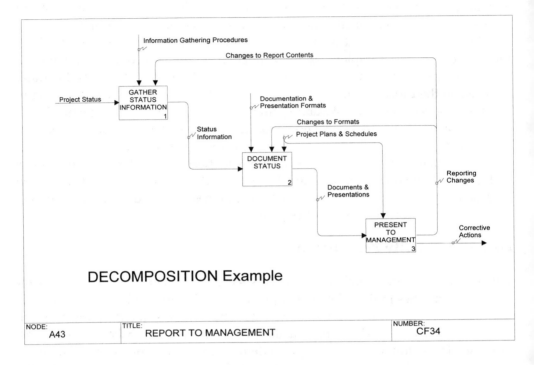

Figure A-2: Decomposition Example.

Document production could be shown as a fourth box (printing, collating, binding, and so on), since it fulfills all of the criteria used to identify the other three boxes. However, the author chose to include this as a sub-function under the document status function. That is, the production of the physical document is a sub-part of the function of documenting the status. It is not worth highlighting at a diagram with node A43's level but is more properly considered a detail of preparing the document as a whole.

The second form of breakdown is *sequential*, which breaks down the parent activity by a sequence of sub-activities. Sequence is popular in process modeling methods, and it is used to describe an event and the subsequent steps of a process to react to the event.

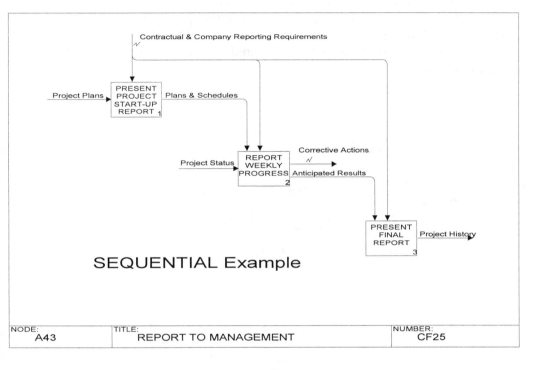

Figure A-3: Sequential Example.

In the example shown in Figure A-3, the author thinks of the order of presenting reports to management, and he breaks down the reporting into three time periods—the initial kick-off meeting, the weekly reporting during project performance, and the final reporting. This author does not decompose the verb "report," but rather, looks at the reporting process as it must be done at different points in time.

Compare this with the decomposition example in Figure A-2, which divides the reporting function into sub-functions of data gathering, report preparation, and presentation. All three documents (start-up documents, weekly documents, and final reporting) are included in the decomposition version, but in Figure A-3, the author presents a sequence of invoking the parent as a breakdown of the single parent function.

The third form of breakdown is *organizational,* in which the breakdown matches the enterprise's organization chart. This form may be useful if one purpose of
the modeling effort is to show the roles and responsibilities of the personnel in an
AS-IS model. However, unless the organization is patterned after the functions to
be performed, the breakdown will be cluttered with many arrows, showing orga-
nization-related interfaces.

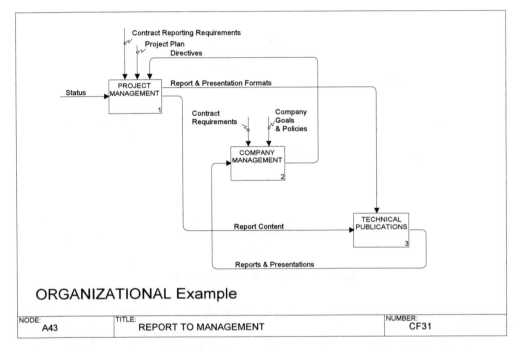

ORGANIZATIONAL Example

NODE: A43	TITLE: REPORT TO MANAGEMENT	NUMBER: CF31

Figure A-4: Organizational Example.

A symptom that reveals to the reader that an organizational breakdown is being
followed is that activity box titles typically contain department names instead of
verb phrases. For example, you might see project management or technical publications as activity titles instead of verb phrases such as MANAGE THE PROJECT or PUB-
LISH THE DOCUMENT.

The danger of using the organizational breakdown form is that the author may
be documenting the existing enterprise structure instead of really analyzing the
enterprise. Another clue that an awkward structure exists is found in the complexity of the arrow structure. That is, if a tangle of arrows seems to be necessary to
represent the breakdown, some of the activities should be clustered together and

the organization should be restructured to reduce internal communication complexity.

In the organizational breakdown diagram of Figure A-4, we see that the TECHNICAL PUBLICATIONS organization is shown at the same level as the other activities, and all of them are depicted as structurally parallel. The data-flow traffic between the boxes is likely to be heavy and not easy to follow when attempting a walk-through. This is one of the most serious reader communication roadblocks—complex arrow structure.

The fourth form of breakdown is *split-by-type* (SBT). Figure A-5 shows the parent activity (REPORT TO MANAGEMENT) applied to different types of topics. The parent activity is not really broken down, but is explored in different situations. This kind of breakdown always results in a diagram with an uninformative arrow pattern, and is better replaced by a call arrow listing the topics or situations and pointing to a separate model for each call arrow reference (see the section treating levels of abstraction in Chapter 3).

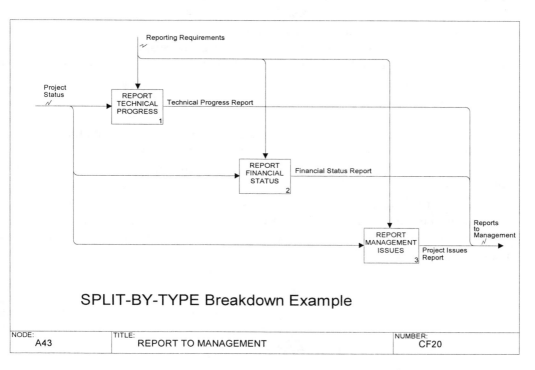

Figure A-5: Split-by-Type Example.

The SBT breakdown in Figure A-5 demonstrates an uninformative arrow pattern in which all three activities are controlled by the reporting requirements, and all three activities use the project status as input. Three types of reports are produced, each of which are merged into the reports to management output.

An inherent danger in using the SBT form of breakdown became evident very early in the application of SADT to process modeling: In modeling a manufacturing process for a complex aerospace product, we found that the part fabrication activity broke down into 28 distinct fabrication processes (milling, sawing, lathe turning, bending, and so on). After considering many ways of grouping the processes into six or fewer activities, we realized that this was a case of SBT: not a decomposition of the verb "to fabricate," but 28 types of fabrication (the parent activity). As a result of this realization, we built separate models for several of the fabrication disciplines and employed a call arrow to list the existing forms of process models.

The SADT example helps us understand the meaning of split-by-type. The breakdown of the verb "to fabricate" applies to all forms of fabrication. Sub-activities using decomposition would result in activities such as START PROCESS, CHECK DURING FABRICATION, EVALUATE ACCURACY, STOP PROCESS, and SIGN ROUTING SLIP. These subprocesses apply to all types of products and processes; they decompose the verb "to process" as it applies to all types of products and part forming. However, to satisfy the purpose of the modeling effort, we should look at specific types of processes (hence the term "split-by-type") rather than analyze the fabrication process in general.

Since this early experience, we have noticed many models that mix the decomposition form of breakdown with the SBT form. They are called a *partial SBT* and can be recognized by the arrow pattern shown in Figure A-5. That is, part of the detail diagram is an SBT and the remainder is a decomposition of the parent activity. If the split is into fewer than six parts, the occurrence of an SBT is often not realized by the author or the commenters. This oversight can be remedied by mounting the complete model on a wall, stepping back, and noting where SBT arrow patterns are evident.

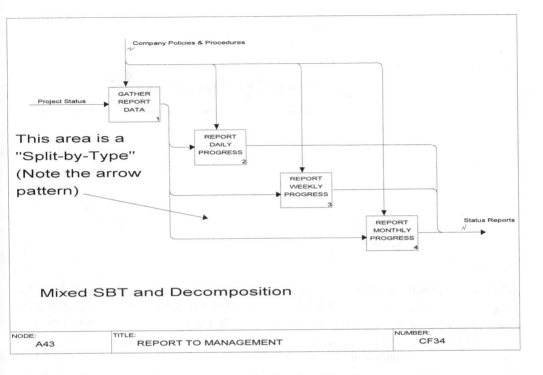

Figure A-6: Partial SBT Example.

Mixing forms of breakdown in a model is generally not a good idea, since it makes the reader switch his way of thinking without warning. The most common form of switching breakdown methods is to include an SBT within a decomposition and then to return to decomposition, as shown in Figure A-6. This typically occurs because the author becomes disinterested in the general level of abstraction and finds it more informative to drop down a level to model specific instances of applying the parent activity. This is clearly a situation in which the call arrow syntax should be applied. To avoid inadvertently switching to the SBT breakdown method, the author should follow the IDEF0 diagramming steps carefully and not skip the initial data list step when beginning a new diagram.

The data listing step helps authors avoid the SBT problem because the mental process of identifying the data elements used or produced by the parent activity, and then of using this list to consider what sub-activities use or produce each data item on the list, naturally leads the author into a decomposition of the parent into its parts. Of course, a drop in level of abstraction may be more helpful to the purpose of the model, and the author must not continue when further decomposition at the present level of abstraction is not helpful.

Appendix B	**Sample Models**

$\blacksquare$his Appendix contains several models that serve as examples of good IDEF0 practice. The first model is the *generic enterprise model* (that is, a model that can be used as the starting point for a wide variety of enterprises). The second is the *AS-IS enterprise model* (baseline for improvement planning), and third is the *configuration management model*.

Most modelers develop several generic models—one for each type of enterprise. Enterprise characteristics that affect how to model content at the top include whether the enterprise is a commercial or governmental enterprise, and whether it provides products or services. To create a generic enterprise model top, model a well-known enterprise and then generalize it by adjusting the box names and arrow labels so that the same diagram can apply to the broadest possible set of enterprises.

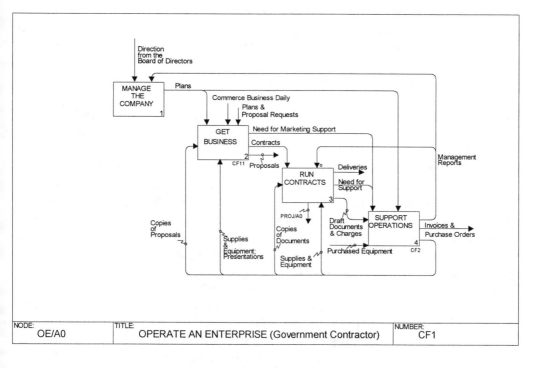

Figure B-1: Candidate Top-Level Generic Enterprise Diagram.

Figure B-1 shows the top diagram of an enterprise model for a government contractor whose area of expertise includes developing DoD software products and
providing technical software-related services to DoD offices. This enterprise provides both products and services, and so the same diagram should apply to both
types of enterprise. Since the products are software, the model may not be relevant to hardware or hybrid products, and we must keep in mind this potential
split. The customer of the enterprise is the DoD, but the model should apply to all
government agencies (Federal Aviation Administration, Census Bureau, and so
forth) since subcontracting to these organizations should be very similar to DoD
subcontracting.

The diagram should apply to commercial enterprises as well as government
subcontractors. To test this hypothesis, we examine each box on the diagram to
see if it pertains to a commercial enterprise, or whether there is some fundamental
function that is missing or extra.

For a diagram to be generic, all of the major elements of an enterprise must be represented, and the box and arrow names must apply to a large variety of enterprises. Furthermore, for the diagram to represent good IDEF0 practice, it must be balanced. That is, each box must represent about the same level of importance to the enterprise as the other boxes; one box cannot be trivial while another is complex.

Figure B-1 shows a candidate top-level generic enterprise diagram. By examining each box in order, we see that an enterprise must have a top-management function (see box 1) to make strategic plans, determine the direction and vision of the enterprise, and manage the enterprise's offices. In a commercial enterprise, a second key element is its marketing and sales function (see box 2). This function is responsible for finding customers, submitting proposals, winning contracts and sales orders, and for continually analyzing market trends and potential new areas of business. At this top level, the model applies to both commercial and government subcontractor enterprises. However, we foresee that this similarity will end when we attempt to decompose the marketing and sales function.

Box 3 represents the primary product or service (technical heart) of the enterprise. This activity provides the principal revenue source for the enterprise. Here, the same function exists in commercial or government subcontractor enterprises, but we anticipate a difference in the model at a fairly general-level breakdown, depending on the type of product or service.

Consider the technical steps required to develop various types of products and services. Clearly, the product design and manufacturing that are needed to produce a hardware product are very different from the less physical activities required to provide a service or develop a software system. Therefore, the next level of breakdown undoubtedly will require a split into hardware product companies versus software and services enterprises. However, the generic approach will need to be applied to at least one more level of decomposition before differences emerge between services and software development enterprises.

Since there is a basic difference in the sub-functions depending on the product or service, the model does not contain a decomposition diagram for box 3. Instead, a call arrow shows that the reader should turn to model "PROJ/A0" for one example of a breakdown of box 3. Other breakdowns may be listed beside the PROJ call arrow in the future, when these alternatives are developed.

Box 4 includes all of the support-level activities of an enterprise. From the input and output arrows, we see that this support includes technical publications and presentations, purchasing and invoicing, management information systems (MIS), contracting, accounting and payroll, and human resources (personnel). All enterprises need these support functions, and by grouping them into a generic support function, the modeler can minimize the unique modeling portion, model the common elements, and apply them to a broad spectrum of enterprises using only a minimum of customization effort.

Here, one may question the diagram's balance, since box 4 and several other boxes include a larger portion of the enterprise than is desirable. The answer to the question, "Should a box be split into several boxes?" depends on the importance of the specific box's activity in pursuing enterprise improvements during BPR. Taking box 4 as an example, we can see that the number of arrows entering and leaving the box is prohibitively large, indicating an unusual amount of back and forth communication between box 4 and the other enterprise functions, thereby making the diagram difficult to understand.

Perhaps business and accounting (serving finance, contracting, and accounting functions), resources (human as well as physical), and publications should replace box 4, becoming boxes 4, 5, and 6. Key questions to ask the management of the enterprise are, "Which version communicates best? Which is most useful for the BPR effort?" Determine whether management considers these support functions as critical to BPR as they are to the enterprise management and marketing and sales functions.

From a purely technical and communications perspective, the change results in a rather complex A0 diagram, but it is more evenly balanced than the prior version. Figure B-2 shows a candidate revised diagram with box 4 split into three parts, as discussed. The choice is left up to the reader as to which version he prefers to use for the top of his enterprise model.

In reviewing these models, consider whether the functions of a generic commercial enterprise model can be applied to government (agency or military) enterprises, since government agencies have different control activities and do not have a marketing element, or whether a generic government enterprise top diagram is needed, which can be applied to a large number of government offices and military organizations.

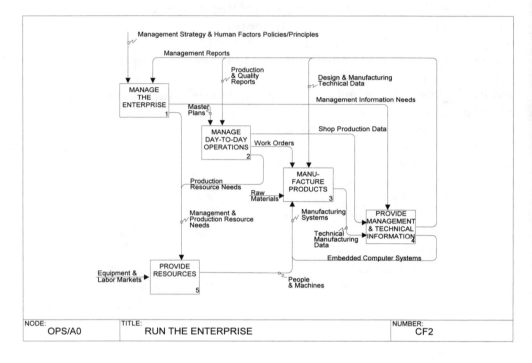

Figure B-2: Alternative Candidate Top-Level Generic Enterprise Diagram.

Figures B-3 through B-12 show an *AS-IS enterprise model,* a sanitized version of an actual BPR AS-IS model that was used to plan improvements in a five-hundred per-son system integration and development firm. With fifteen field offices across the United States, the firm services the Department of Defense as its largest market. These models illustrate the use of IDEF0 discussed in the main body of this book.

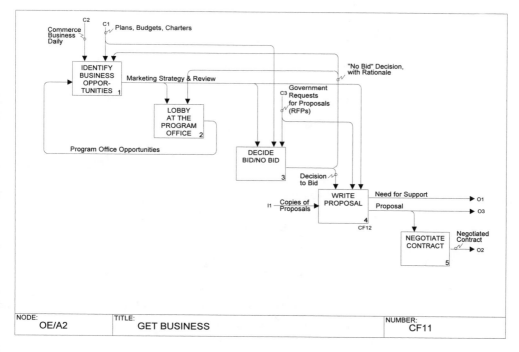

Figure B-3: AS-IS Enterprise Model.

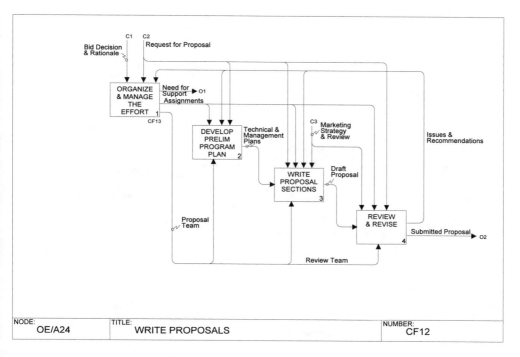

Figure B-4: AS-IS Enterprise Model.

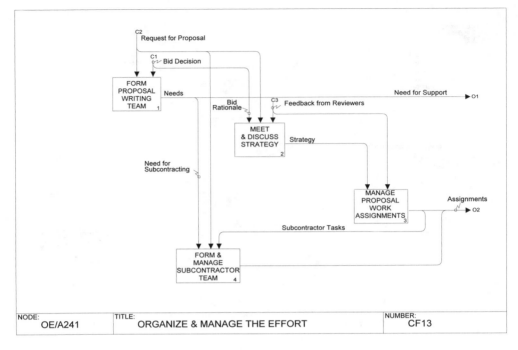

Figure B-5: AS-IS Enterprise Model.

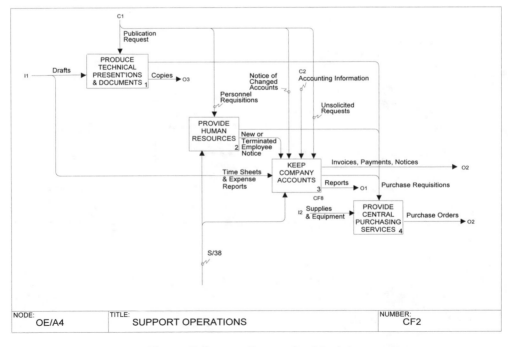

Figure B-6: AS-IS Enterprise Model.

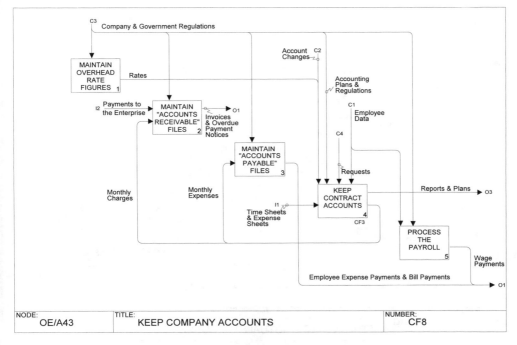

Figure B-7: AS-IS Enterprise Model.

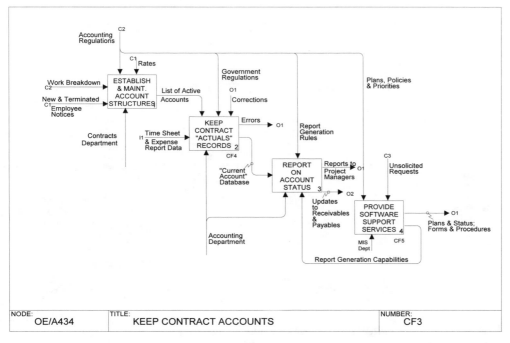

Figure B-8: AS-IS Enterprise Model.

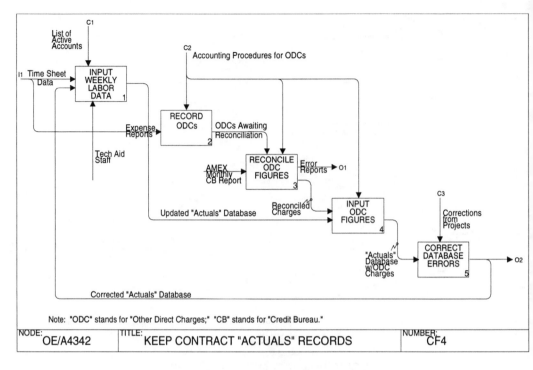

Figure B-9: AS-IS Enterprise Model.

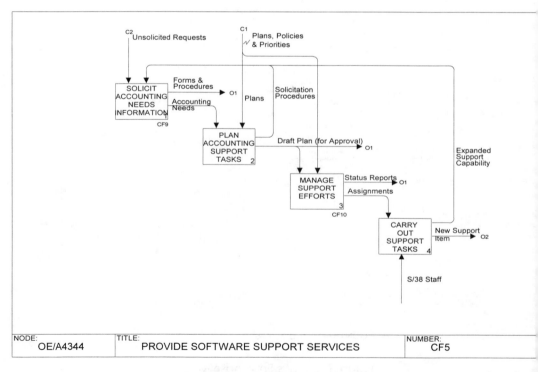

Figure B-10: AS-IS Enterprise Model.

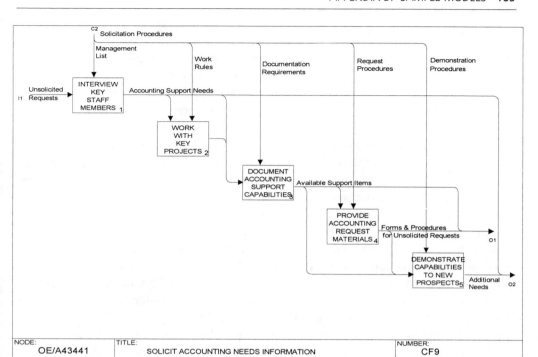

Figure B-11: AS-IS Enterprise Model.

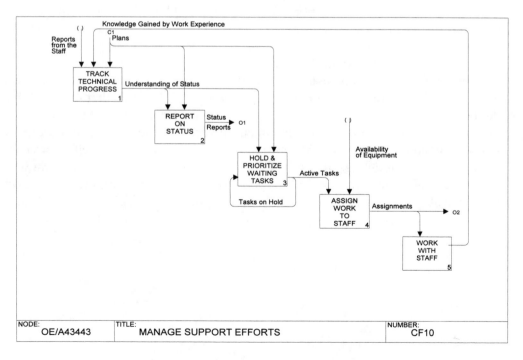

Figure B-12: AS-IS Enterprise Model.

In Figure B-13 we have a *configuration management model*, a one-diagram summary of the military standard MIL-STD-483A for software configuration management, illustrating a function-oriented breakdown in which each box represents a unique functional aspect of software configuration management. That is, the job of software configuration management consists of the five kinds of activities shown in the boxes: planning, identifying the pieces of the system, maintaining baseline versions of the system, providing status accounting reports to project management, and controlling and recording changes. No matter when one of these types of activities occurs, the box shown on the diagram is activated.

This figure contrasts to a process or timing-based breakdown in which activities that happen at different points in time (perhaps employing different staff) are shown in separate boxes. This model is particularly useful for pinpointing staff responsibilities and variations in the process that depend on the time at which the process is invoked (for example, initial design, detailed design, or design change).

The function-based diagram of Figure B-13 is clearly much more concise than the ten process-based diagrams used in Figures B-3 through B-12 to cover the same topic. The function-based diagram, the original form for an IDEF0 and SADT model, has the additional advantage that similarities of activations are identified, and a single support system can be developed that satisfies all the requirements of the function, whenever and whoever performs the function (for example, a single design system for all phases of design).

The model includes annotations on the arrows and below the boxes that identify paragraph numbers in various military standards, so that the reader may review the configuration management functions as well as turn to the referenced paragraph to see the detailed definition, arrow contents, or process requirements.

The final example consists of four diagrams (Figures B-14 through B-17) extracted from a configuration manager's view of his job. Note that the functions defined in the functional version (Figure B-13) are included here, but that the activities include coordination with development projects, providing snapshot copies of selected versions of systems as requested. This model illustrates the effect of viewpoint on IDEF0 modeling. It resulted from actual interviews with the configuration management manager and his experience in providing support to a project involving about fifty programmers in the development of a large software system.

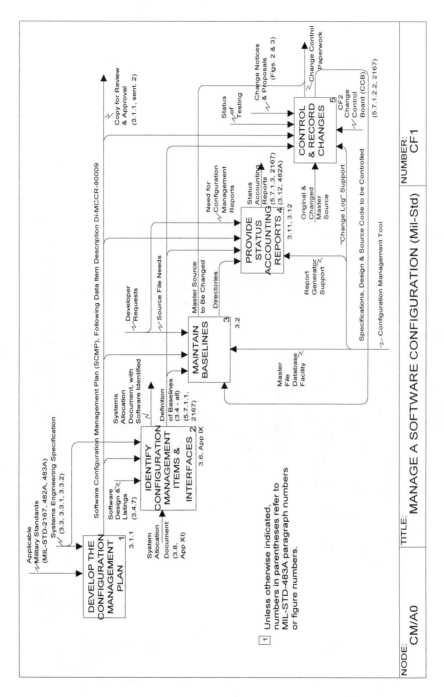

Figure B-13: Configuration Management Model.

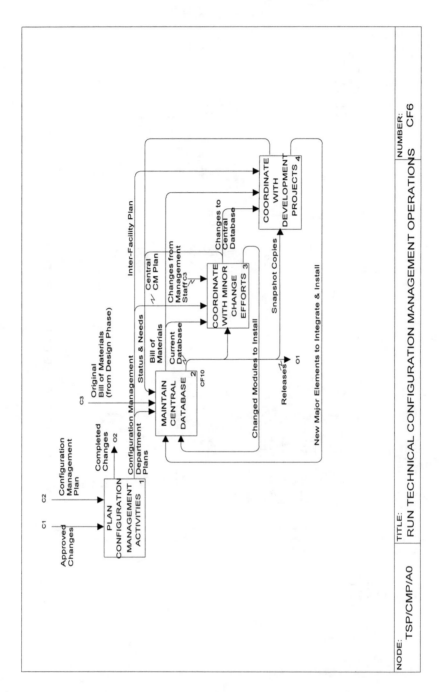

Figure B-14: Configuration Manager's View.

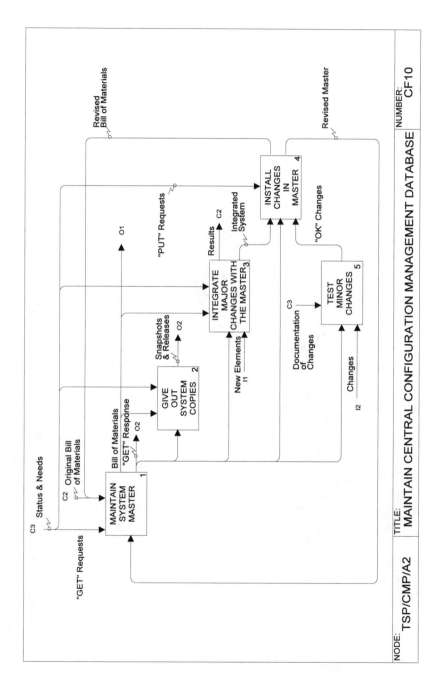

Figure B-15: Configuration Manager's View.

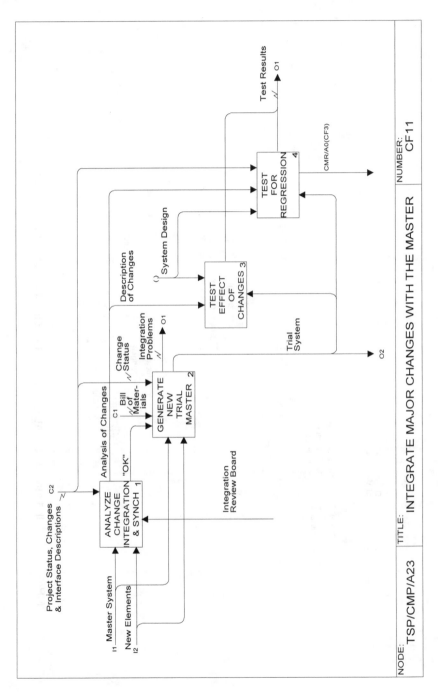

Figure B-16: Configuration Manager's View.

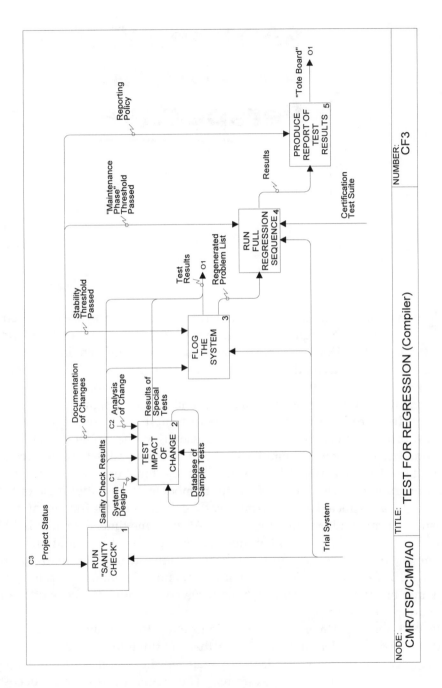

Figure B-17: Configuration Manager's View.

SADT and IDEF0—
A Historical Perspective

Appendix
C

A s mentioned in Chapter 1, Structured Analysis and Design Technique
(SADT) is the original and highly rigorous structured analysis approach
invented by Douglas T. Ross, then Chairman of SofTech, Inc. First used in
the U.S. Air Force's 1973 AFCAM Project, SADT is the archetype of system blue-
printing methods, providing an engineering method for performing and managing
requirements definition, functional analysis, and system design.

From its introduction as the architecture method proposed for use in the
AFCAM program on computer-aided manufacturing, the structured analysis (SA)
modeling language of SADT emphasized both activity and data parts, recognizing
the need for definitive modeling of arbitrary subject matter. Toward the end of the
ICAM program in 1978, most of the activity modeling of SA (but none of the data
modeling) was extracted as IDEF0 and was recommended for functional modeling
of manufacturing and business processes. At the same time, the name IDEF1 was
applied to a non-SA, entity-attribute-relationship-based information modeling
scheme for data definition and database design. It later was supplanted by
IDEF1X. IDEF2, for behavioral modeling, was not adequate to win a significant
following, but IDEF0 and IDEF1X have received the primary focus of the IDEF0
User Group membership.

In 1991, the Department of Defense, in its effort to cut military spending, identified IDEF0 as a golden nugget. Rather than continue to build new systems, the
DoD emphasized business practices and analyzed site operations for potential cost
savings and reuse of existing systems. The IDEF0 process was successfully

applied by the Army Corps of Engineers and, in early 1992, was adopted by the Corporate Information Management (CIM) Policy Committee as a standard.

Comparison of SADT with IDEF0

The IDEF0 technique is a subset of SADT that was extracted and packaged by SofTech, Inc., at the behest of the ICAM Project Office, and then was adopted by the Air Force ManTech Office and others as the mandated method to be used in many procurements and projects. Fortunately, the syntax and semantics of IDEF0 are identical to the equivalent portion of SADT. Therefore, there is no conflict between users of the two methods, and support tools exist for common features. In an effort to simplify elementary use of the method and improve its prospects for adoption, the Air Force required that many useful features of SADT be omitted from the IDEF0 subset. Among the features excluded were

1. data modeling (properly *dual* to activity modeling)
2. two-way arrows and other syntax features
3. activation language and Q-labels (quantification)
4. rigorously derived model presentation forms (for example, schematics)
5. the tie process to rigorously relate models to each other and to other data and document forms

Let us look at just one of these: Q-labels provide the foundation for simulation in SADT models, since they quantify processing times, labor resources, and so on. Figure C-1 shows an example of an SADT diagram with Q-label quantification.

The figure shows activity 1 and activity 2 looping an average number of times, and then producing 2O1. Activity 3 requires an average time of (x) hours to process each 3I1, with a specified size of staff. Finally, the flow rate per day emerging from activity 4 is indicated, along with the number of staff required for the processing.

This type of quantification labeling is created as a for-exposition-only (FEO) diagram, with unnecessary labels omitted (for example, there are no controls shown on activities 3 and 4, since they are not necessary for the quantification analysis). It has been successfully used for high-level simulation on several military projects, including a Navy project to simulate shipboard fire control. In that project, the lowest-level SADT activities were actually programmed in Ada, and the resulting simulator was used to evaluate new Navy software.

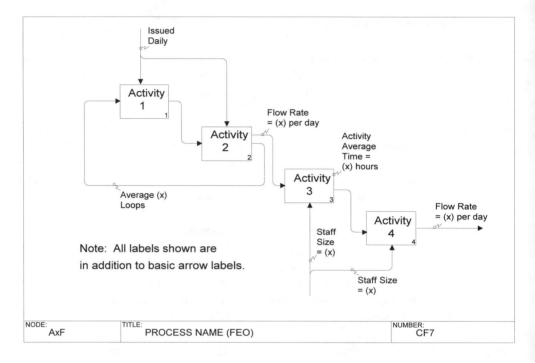

Figure C-1: Diagram with Q-Label Quantification.

The SADT features that were omitted when IDEF0 was defined have caused analysts to turn to other methods to develop the information they need. Specifically, Q-labels are needed to perform cost and timing analysis. Activation rules are needed to simulate the model.

The concepts of data modeling in SADT have recently been related to object modeling concepts. An effort is under way to compare the use of SADT data modeling to object models. If this effort is successful, considerable cost and time could be saved by eliminating the need to rework SADT and IDEF0 models for object-oriented software development, as is now envisioned.

Present users of IDEF0 are pursuing the potential for revisiting these features of SADT. The forum for such efforts is provided by the ISEE (International Society for Enterprise Engineering) and by NIST (National Institute of Standards and Technology).

SADT Data Models, IDEF0, and IDEF1X

Appendix D

S ADT data modeling is closely related to activity modeling. With a data model, the entire system is modeled top-down, but this time the data elements are represented by boxes that are decomposed into subcategories of the parent data group. The activities become the arrows that show how the data is created and used. The control arrows become the activities that control how the data is called for or used. The mechanism becomes the device that holds the data (database and storage device).

Data decomposition of an SADT data model shows the enterprise's data from a top-down perspective and identifies which activities directly use and create each data element. In this way, an SADT data model represents a dynamic view of the creation and use of enterprise data. This type of analysis graphically depicts the activities that are affected by a change in a data element—a key aspect of controlling change.

An IDEF1X model captures the relationships between individual data elements, the attributes of each element, and the means of identifying each element. If a data element has a discrete set of instantiations, these may also be displayed (such as the types of products produced by the enterprise).

Thus, the SADT data model and the IDEF1X data model complement each other; one shows the dynamics of data creation and usage, and the other shows the attributes and relationships of the data.

SADT data models are organized in a hierarchical, top-down decomposition structure similar to an SADT or IDEF0 activity breakdown. However, there is no concept of hierarchy in IDEF1X—the model is a large chart with possibly hundreds of individual data items depicted. SADT data models employ the "gradual exposition of detail" feature to aid communication, whereas IDEF1X data models define in precise detail, so that data may be processed by a computer.

Experts disagree over which form of analysis should be done first. Because of the communication power of IDEF0, users typically opt for activity analysis first. That is, it is easier for users to consider groups of activities and organization structures than to see the forest for the trees in a large IDEF1X data model.

The decision partly depends on the type of system to be analyzed. For example, a banking system typically deals with very simple transactions (adding money to accounts, transferring funds, and so on), and the most important area to analyze is the massive data-handling effort involved in these applications. On the other hand, a complex manufacturing process is concerned with processes, rather than the short-lived intermediate data passed between workstations.

Another key aspect relating to sequencing is the ability to provide needed results in the most efficient way, in the shortest possible time, and at the least cost. Those who prefer to start with data analysis argue that integration can only be accomplished if the enterprise has a well-structured data infrastructure and that an analyst cannot begin to make meaningful progress until the enterprise's terminology is clarified.

These are telling points, but activity analysts argue that you must have the processes understood and optimized before it makes sense to optimize the data. It does no good to optimize data that is not useful. Also, many forms of improvement (the introduction of Total Quality Management, the elimination of non-value-added tasks, or the introduction of new technology, for example) are only accomplished through careful analysis of the enterprise's processes.

When starting the analysis of an enterprise, the first thing a modeler needs to accomplish is to define the terminology commonly used by the enterprise. Both IDEF0 and IDEF1X recognize this fact: The starting point of an IDEF0 model is to list and define the data elements at the top of the structure; the starting point of an IDEF1X analysis is to document the business rules either in a form of structured English or in IDEF1X entity-attribute-relationship form.

It clearly is overkill at the outset to define a complete, fully attributed data model, so the common procedure is to capture key entities and relationships, without worrying about solving many-to-many relationships, defining keys, or listing attributes at this early stage. The equivalent starting point for the activity analysis is to build a data dictionary so that meaningful interviews can be held to define the top-level diagrams of the model.

Since the same enterprise is being modeled in both cases, it is not surprising that the resultant models are related. Figure D-1 illustrates an IDEF0 activity box and arrow set and its relation to an IDEF1X model of the same area.

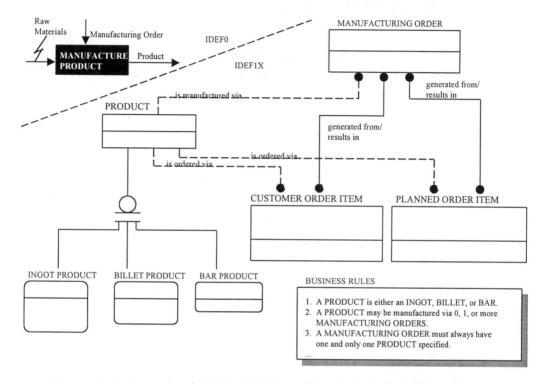

Figure D-1: Example of IDEF0, IDEF1X, and Business Rule Relationship.

An IDEF0 activity box (MANUFACTURE PRODUCT) is shown in the upper-left corner of the figure. Upon inspection, the output arrow Product appears to be related to the IDEF1X PRODUCT box, which shows the three types of products and their attributes. Likewise, the IDEF0 control arrow identifies Manufacturing Order as the control of the process, whereas the IDEF1X model breaks out the major elements of a MANU-FACTURING ORDER.

The two models complement each other and provide needed detail for the analysis. In the IDEF0 case, the information is gained by interviewing experts and creating a data dictionary for the terms "product" and "manufacturing order." In IDEF1X, the business rules are captured in a form of structured English (see bottom-right corner of the figure) and then modeled as IDEF1X graphics by the data analyst (center of the figure).

In conclusion, the consensus is that some amount of process modeling should be done first before data modeling. Once the operational details of the enterprise are well understood, the time will come when an in-depth analysis using IDEF1X is essential. The statement is often made that "the key to an integrated, agile enterprise is integration of the information of the enterprise." This is correct. However, the corollary should be stated: "Once the enterprise's processes are optimized, there must be an integrated information infrastructure to achieve the benefits and provide the information needed to operate and control the enterprise."

Appendix
E

A Modeling Process
Case Study

he following study of Ben's Burgers is based on the model of a small restaurant chain. The example is used in an IDEF0 workshop to teach students how to develop IDEF0 models. It is designed to provide practice in developing an IDEF0 model, and it describes a realistic environment that is typical of what will be encountered in real environments. The information is presented as an interview with the owner of the restaurant chain who details his ideas for improvements. Your job is to listen, model the AS-IS operation, and identify as many improvements as possible, including those originally expressed by the owner. You may also wish to provide a TO-BE model showing a vision of future operations.

Background of the Restaurant

Ben's Burgers is a chain of twenty restaurants located in New Jersey. They serve basic fast-food fare: hamburgers, hot dogs, fries, sodas. Most of the locations provide indoor seating, but a few are small take-out facilities with a walk-up window and a few picnic tables. Most of the restaurants also have a drive-through window.

The restaurant chain has experienced tremendous growth in the past few years, and Ben is fast losing control of the information he needs to maintain in order to expand his operations further. He is also losing the close contact with his customers that characterized his restaurant chain and was in a significant way responsible for his success.

Ben's background before opening the restaurant chain has had an influence on his outlook. He left an executive position with a major airline to found Ben's Burgers. Therefore, he has seen how information technology can be a critical component of an enterprise. Because of this, he wants to use information technology in as much of his operation as possible, so long as the automation does not negatively impact the quality of his food or the service he provides to his customers.

Excerpt from an Interview with the President and CEO

Ben: "I started nine years ago selling burgers, hot dogs, fries, and sodas out of a stand in downtown Princeton. The place had four parking spaces, two picnic tables, and no indoor seating. I'm sure you've seen lots of places like that one. It turns out that a good burger at a good price is just what Princeton needed, because we could barely make them fast enough. So I leased a small restaurant down the block and added a few menu items, but kept the same basic business plan. A good burger, cooked just the way the customer wants it, with all the fixin's or none of them, whatever the customer wants.

"One of the things that made us successful in the early days was that I made an effort to remember our customers and how they liked their burgers. I took pride in remembering if they liked them medium rare, with onions and lettuce, or well done with lots of ketchup—that sort of thing. People like to be recognized and remembered. Of course, now with twenty restaurants in the area, we have lost that. Most people don't have my knack for remembering faces. Jeff Shermon has some ideas in this area, but I'll let you talk to him about them later.

"Each manager currently has his own tracking system. Things like orders, deliveries, and payments are tracked. It just takes me too darn long to review what is going on with twenty slightly different systems in place. I want one computer system that everyone can use so that they all are doing things more or less the same way, or at least so that I can see the numbers easier than I can see them today. In fact, I spent all morning trying to review the orders from the Morristown store. The guy is a good manager, but his handwriting is impossible. Turned out everything was in order, but I just don't have the time to struggle with stuff like this anymore. I need it right at my fingertips.

"That's where we've been and where we are today. Here's where I want to go. Even though we are relatively small, I am spending way too much time on administrative duties like ordering, evaluating suppliers and restaurants, payroll, and things like that. I have played with the numbers, and I believe that if Ben's Burgers makes an investment in information technology now, I will save myself and my employees a whole lot of time. Also, I think I will be able to make better decisions about how my managers are doing at each location, what items should be advertised, and things like that.

"I think I need a central computer at the corporate office here, plus at least one PC at each store. This way, they can all share the same information and I can track all the stores in a consistent way.

"Here is one problem that I'm having that I think can be improved by putting some type of information system in place. I am committed to Ben's Burgers always using the finest, freshest ingredients I can get my hands on. Currently, all of the restaurants do their own ordering—chopped meat, lettuce, ketchup—things like that. This has resulted in two problems: First, I am not getting the volume discounts that I could be getting if we had some type of central ordering system; second, I've caught a few of my managers ordering second-rate ingredients from suppliers I don't want to deal with. Some of my managers tend to focus too much on short-term profits. They figure if they can save a nickel a burger on beef, their numbers will look better. I want them to spend the extra nickel and keep the customer. Basically, I need some type of integrated ordering and payment system. This way I can easily ensure that orders and checks only go to approved vendors for the products they are approved to supply.

"Another problem is a result of giving store managers a lot of freedom when it comes to putting new items on the menu. The problem is that when one of the items is a big success at one restaurant, the others start selling the new menu item—but each restaurant starts making it a little differently. For example, here is what happened when the Trenton restaurant came up with the idea for a big sandwich, a quarter pound of beef with a slice of onion on top. They called it a Big Ben. Well, it sold so well that other stores started picking it up. Problem was, a customer that got one with a big raw onion in Trenton would get one with grilled onions in Princeton and one with no onions in Wayne. What I need is a record of standard menu items. If more than one store has something on the menu, they all have to make it the same.

"Talk to Jeff Shermon. Jeff is in charge of opening new stores. He is also my right-hand man on special projects and new ideas. Jeff was my third employee, right after the first short-order cook. He started out picking up garbage in the parking lot and in no time at all he was ordering supplies, managing the order takers, and helping me open new stores. In the early days, Jeff was the company. In any case, he has an idea of how we could get some of the customer recognition back that we had in the old days. I want you to talk to him. I don't know if I can afford to implement all of his ideas, but I want you to be aware of them, so that they can be easily added later."

Excerpt from an Interview with Jeff Shermon

Jeff: "Okay. Here is my idea. In the old days, Ben knew just about everybody who walked up to the counter. It was amazing. 'Hi, Bob. That'll be a cheeseburger, well done, with a large orange soda, right?' I think that was a big part of Ben's Burgers' success. Obviously we can't do that anymore, so what I would like to do is give our customers a Ben Card, just like an ATM card. When we give one to a customer, we have him fill out a form with his preferences—things like how he likes the burger, how much ketchup, what size fries, with or without onion—things like that. Before a customer places his order, we would have him run his card through a card-reader machine, and the person taking the order will have all of the knowledge in front of him that Ben used to have in his head. Not only that, but we will be able to offer bonuses to our frequent customers, just like the airlines.

"Also, Ben thinks that if we had a record of common orders, we could do a better job of offering and advertising packaged meals. If we find that people who order fish sandwiches don't usually order fries, we don't want to advertise a special featuring those two things together. If, on the other hand, it turns out that people who order big drinks also tend to order big fries, we will probably want to come up with some kind of special that makes those folks think they're getting a good buy."

Modeling Ben's Burgers

Notes from the interview should be used as source material for modeling the business. The seven basic modeling steps are presented in Figure E-1.

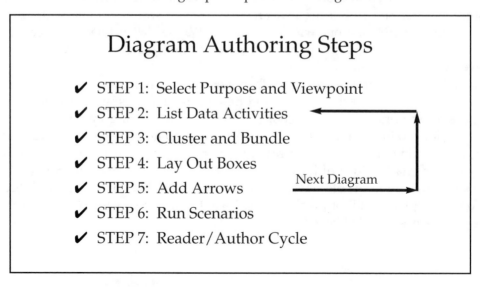

Figure E-1: Diagram Authoring Steps.

After selecting the purpose and viewpoint of the model (step 1), the author develops a set of diagrams, looping through steps 2 through 5 until there is sufficient model to run the scenario (step 6), and then to conduct the reader/author cycle (step 7). The process begins again at step 2, until the model is complete.

The following nine diagrams (Figures E-2 through E-10) present an overview of step 1 and a detail-oriented breakdown of the overview. As the first step in creating a model, select the purpose and viewpoint. In modeling Ben's Burgers, we have several candidates.

First, prepare an AS-IS model to show how the restaurant chain now operates. The problems troubling the president may be better understood if modeled, rather than being left vague and unclear. Furthermore, some of the reasons behind the way things now work may not be obvious to the president, and a detailed picture of the present operation may explain away the mystery. Figure E-2 suggests possible approaches.

Step 1: Select Purpose and Viewpoint

✔ Potential Purposes: ✔ Potential Viewpoints:

Develop a Baseline AS-IS Model   Management

→ to identify and define   Customer
  problems
                                   Supplier
→ to analyze potential
  improvements   Accountant

→ to plan introduction   Finance Officer
  of new technology
                                   Information Specialist

                                   Production Supervisor

                                   Quality Assurance

Figure E-2: Step 1, Purpose and Viewpoint.

Certainly, if a new system is to replace the existing order and tracking systems, we must not overlook important features and thus inadvertently reduce the functionality available to the managers. Events and records that now provide important information must be matched or replaced by an equivalent or better feature in the new system, or managers will be reluctant to use the new system.

Select Purpose (Continued)

Develop a TO-BE Model Baseline

→ to plan improvement projects

→ to set vision and goals for the enterprise

→ to communicate and gain consensus on plans

→ to estimate benefits (cost, time, and so on)

→ to identify roles and responsibilities

→ to facilitate training in new operations

→ to analyze controls, communications, and so on

Figure E-3: Select Purpose, Continued.

After step 1, you should have an AS-IS model you are satisfied with. Next, develop a TO-BE model, which will show how the operation will work after implementation of the improvements (see Figure E-3). This TO-BE model allows the analyst to capture the business owner's vision of the future operation. Furthermore, the author can demonstrate the business owner's plans for the future by conducting reader reviews and walkthroughs with the staff. Consensus can be reached so that all personnel are supportive of the change. Such a model serves as a baseline against which to estimate cost and time savings to be derived under the improved operation. It also serves as a valuable training aid for new staff and for retraining current staff.

Select Purpose (Continued)

Develop a "Migration" Project Model

→ to show the tasks to achieve TO-BE from AS-IS

→ to estimate effort, cost, and time to achieve a TO-BE operation

→ to provide a baseline for a project plan (or several project plans)

→ to identify project roles and responsibilities

Figure E-4: Select Purpose, Continued.

Next, develop a project model, which depicts the tasks to be performed to evolve from the AS-IS to the TO-BE operation. It forms the basis of the project plan, which also includes schedules, definition of deliverables, and so on. Roles and responsibilities are also shown as mechanisms, with accompanying text to spell out specific responsibilities of each participant. The project plan may also be used to estimate the cost and time required to implement the changes, using an activity-based costing (ABC) approach. This is done by estimating the time required to process each activity box, the number of times each box will be activated, and the number of personnel required to perform the task.

Select Purpose (Continued)

✔ Other Purposes:

Define user interfaces to new IS support

Analyze functional requirements for new IS

Model alternative changes and compare

Provide the top-level design of a new IS

Introduce new concepts (such as TQM)

Analyze human factors of the enterprise

Figure E-5: Select Purpose, Continued.

Other reasons to create the TO-BE model include providing a precise definition of the user interface to the new information system, analyzing functional requirements and their cost, considering alternatives and new ideas, and considering the human factors that often make or break the new system. (For example, the human factors include the willingness of the users to make proper use of the new system.)

Selected Purpose Statement

"This model will be used to analyze potential improvements, including the development of a central ordering and tracking system."

Figure E-6: Statement of Purpose.

The selected purpose statement for model development is presented in Figure E-6. The statement is worded to specify the primary goal—in this case, developing the new ordering and tracking system—but also to leave the door open for potential improvements that come up in the process of modeling the AS-IS picture. The implications of the selected purpose is that the model

- Acknowledges the current operation detail by
  - ❑ retaining useful elements
  - ❑ demanding precise definition of IS requirements
  - ❑ defining needed user interfaces
- Dictates the approach to decomposition

The viewpoint needed to model Ben's Burgers must be representative of those people responsible for areas of improvement—the managers (see Figure E-7). Thus, we will not focus on the customers, the preparation of the burgers themselves, or the like, but rather will focus on the business aspects of the operation.

Selected Viewpoint

Enterprise Management

Figure E-7: Selected Viewpoint.

We select the model viewpoint to represent all restaurant management, including the president of Ben's Burgers and all individual restaurant managers.

Now that the purpose and viewpoint have been selected, review the interview notes and list all of the *data* items mentioned in the interview. After studying this data-oriented list, list all *activities* that make use of the data items or that indicate new ones to be created. (See Figure E-8.)

Step 2: List Data and Activities

✔ **Data List**

    restaurants
    indoor seating
    walk-up window
    picnic tables
    drive-through window
    fast food
    freshness
    price
    quality and service
    business plan
    customer preferences
    tracking system
    orders
    deliveries
    payments
    advertisements
    short-term profits

✔ **Activity List**

    sell burgers
    track
    order supplies
    develop menus
    open new stores
    administrate
    order
    evaluate supplies and restaurants
    make payments
    improve product
    improve service

Figure E-8: Step 2, List Data and Activities.

Eleven activities resulted from the analysis shown in Figure E-8, but IDEF0 rules tell us we must next cluster them to reduce the number to six or fewer. Since we are doing a functional decomposition, the first consideration is to look for functional similarities and activities that are of interest to the selected viewpoint. Also, are any of the activities very much simpler than others on the list? If so, these are good candidates for clustering.

Step 3: Cluster Activities and Bundle Data

Cluster no more than six activities:

→ look for functional similarities
→ aim for balance of complexity
→ emphasize activities of interest to the Viewpoint and serving the Purpose

Create pipelines of data:

→ level of generality to match activities
→ group by common purpose/use

Figure E-9: Step 3, Cluster and Bundle.

Once the activity list is clustered, look again at the data item list and bundle the data elements to match the level of generality of the new set of activities. Again, individual data items that are functionally similar should be bundled, reducing the model to fewer pipelines.

As an exercise, cluster the Activity List in Figure E-8 to six or fewer activities of approximately the same complexity. Then—without peeking first!—compare your new set with those in Figure E-10.

Results of Clustering and Bundling

✔ Data Bundles

Restaurants (existing and
new facilities)
Fast food (ingredients,
orders, suppliers, pay-
ments)
Quality and service (cus-
tomer preferences, fresh-
ness, price, suppliers)
Business plan (growth,
expansion, public
image)
Tracking system (orders,
deliveries, payments)
Local manager concerns
(short-term profits, top
management, success
criteria)

✔ Activity Clusters

Serve customers (sell burgers, improve product
and service)
Manage local restaurant
(track supply orders,
develop menus, improve
local product and ser-
vice)
Provide supplies (order supplies, improve product)
Oversee business operations
(track, administrate,
improve product and
service)
Expand the business (open
new stores, improve
product and business)

Figure E-10: Results of Clustering and Bundling.

This last step of clustering represents the heart of the analysis—the capability of the analyst to see similarities and to bundle separate activities into more general groupings. Actually, each person attempting to do this will most likely come up with a different set of activity clusters and data bundles. The key is to identify activities of a level of complexity and interest that suits the purpose of the model and the selected viewpoint. Remember that the entire enterprise must be shown in the model, but only the activities and data that accomplish the model's purpose are emphasized. Of course, only those activities that relate to the model's purpose need be decomposed. The rest can remain at the general level and serve as an overview of the big picture.

Step 4: Lay Out Boxes

✔ Arrange boxes in a stairstep fashion

✔ Organize boxes by dominance

✔ Enter name in definition (box number is added automatically)

Figure E-11: Step 4, Lay Out Boxes.

When you are satisfied with the lists of activities and data, sketch the first attempt at a diagram by laying out the boxes in a stairstep fashion. You may change the order later, but the dominance of the boxes should guide the positioning of the activities in the stairstep. (Recall that the dominant boxes generate arrows that control the less dominant boxes.) Figure E-12 shows one possible first diagram.

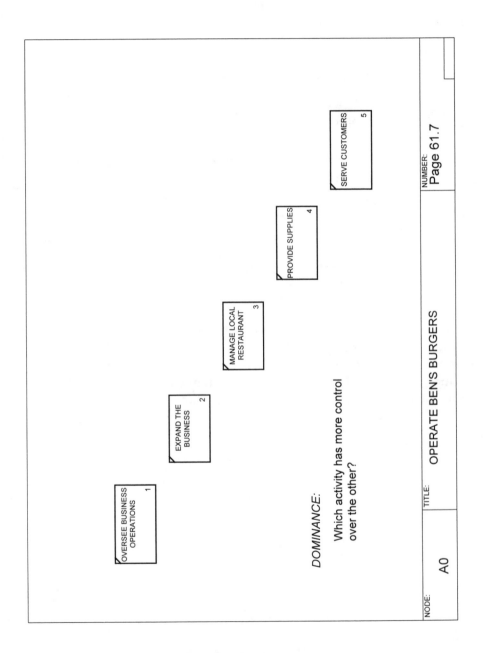

Figure E-12: Operate Ben's Burgers.

Figure E-13 shows step 5, the way to add arrows to the model. After referring to the list of bundled arrows, connect the boxes (see Figure E-13). First, draw the main path; then, add other interfaces. Consider each activity regarding its various activations: What if incorrect data are included in an input arrow? What feedback is provided to other activities? What individual events could trigger the activity?

Step 5: Add Arrows

✔ Use list of bundled arrows

✔ Draw main path

✔ Draw other interfaces

✔ Consider each activity for feedback

✔ Check off arrow list to be sure all data are used

✔ Clean up context arrows

Figure E-13: Step 5, Add Arrows.

Before completing the diagram, the data list is again reviewed to see where each data item is used on the diagram. Finally, review the parent diagram (if any) to see what story was implied. Does the new diagram reflect the same story? In other words, will the reader be surprised when he sees the new diagram versus what he was expecting? The added material is shown in the next five diagrams.

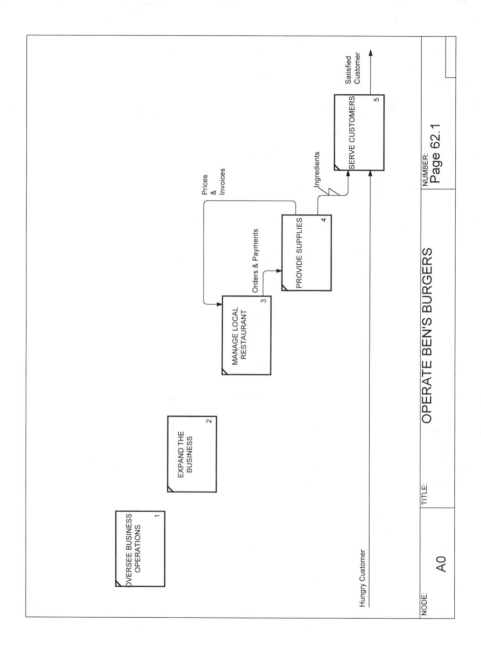

Figure E-14: Operate Ben's Burgers.

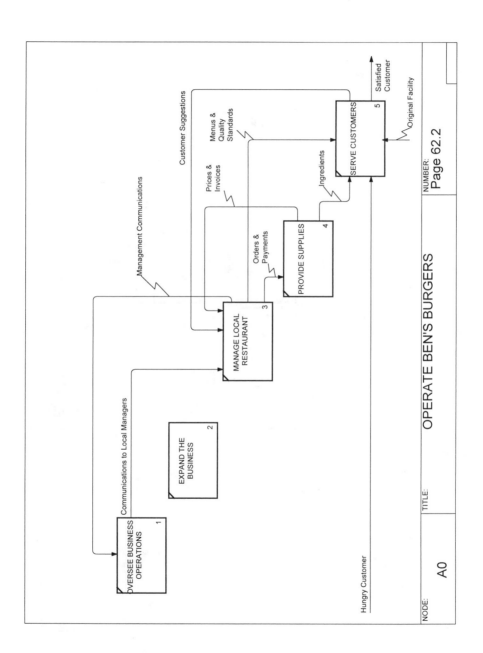

Figure E-15: Operate Ben's Burgers.

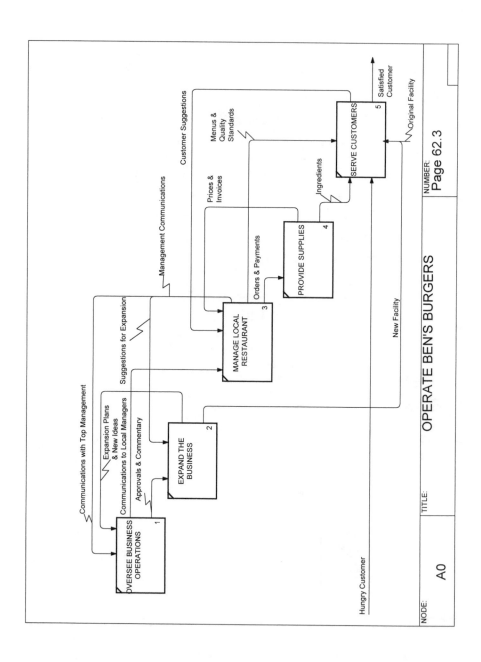

Figure E-16: Operate Ben's Burgers.

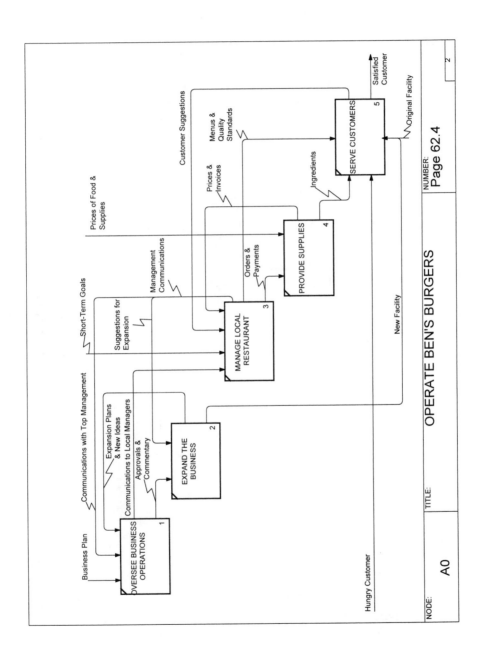

Figure E-17: Operate Ben's Burgers.

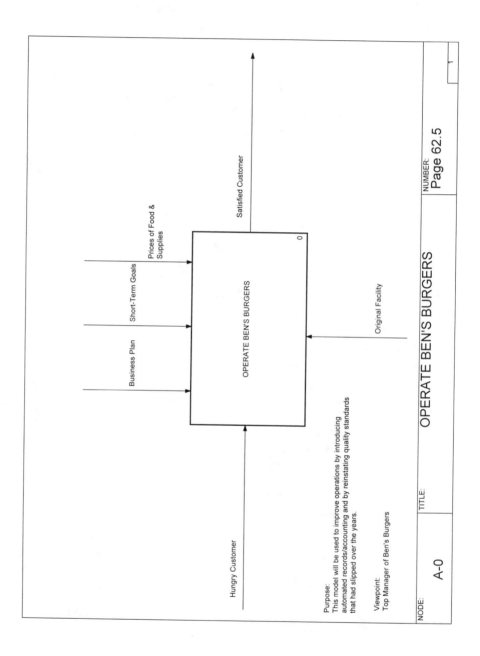

Figure E-18: Operate Ben's Burgers.

The purpose of the model was to help design the improvements in the restaurant operation. Is there information in the interview notes that is not yet evident on the diagram? Since we generalized the activities and the data pipelines, it is likely that we need to decompose one or more of the activities to bring out the level of detail contained in the interview notes. The questions to be asked are

- Do we have enough detail?
- Does the diagram include sufficient detail to serve the purpose?
- Are there questions that cannot be answered from diagram detail?

Our review shows that we do need to provide more detail regarding the current ordering and tracking process, since this will be the basis of the new information system requirements specification that we are to provide.

To identify which activities should be decomposed, we need to select the most revealing box for the model's purpose. In our current scenario, we need to ask where tracking, ordering, and payment are currently. The answer is, activity 3 (MANAGE LOCAL RESTAURANT), which discusses how individual managers run the restaurants. This activity focuses on the individual stores' methods for ordering and tracking, details which will be essential if a central system is created.

The next step is to decompose activity 3 using the same sequence as above.

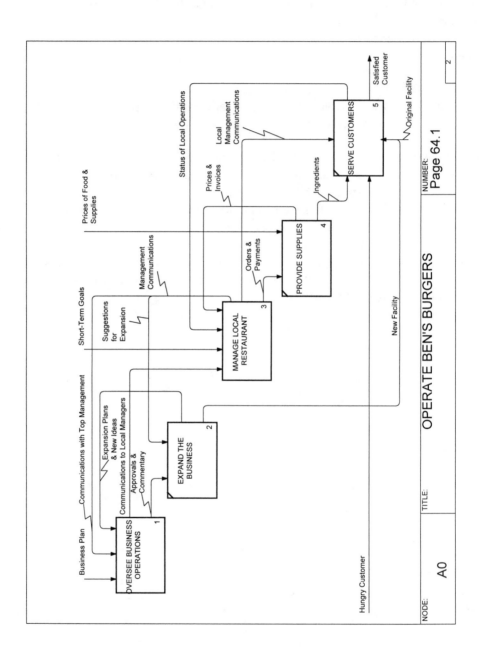

Figure E-19: Operate Ben's Burgers.

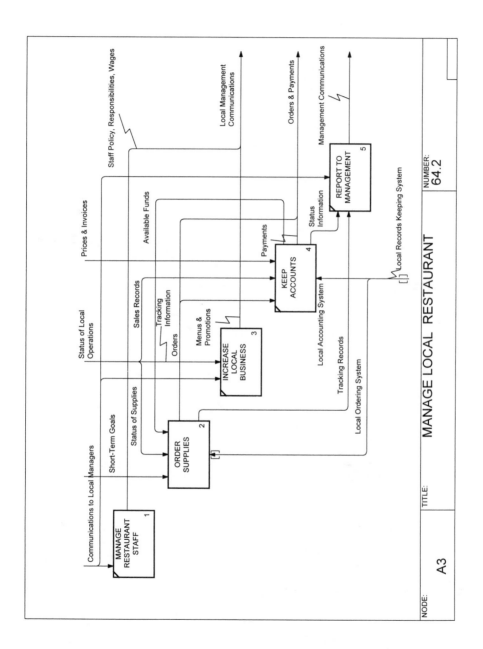

Figure E-20: Manage Local Restaurant.

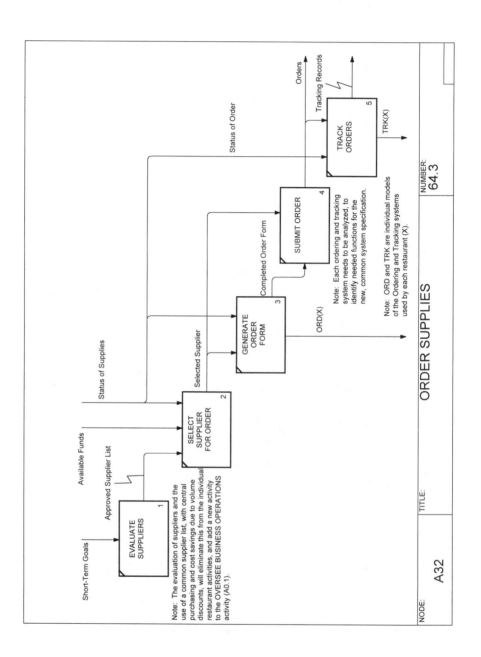

Figure E-21: Order Supplies.

After decomposing activity 3, using the same procedure as with the first diagram, we now decide that there is sufficient detail about the present process to get on with designing the new corporate system. To validate our understanding, we then prepare to run a reader/author review cycle with the experts that were interviewed. But before sending them a copy of the model, we owe it to them to do one final check to catch any errors and oversights. This is the "cleanup" step in which we determine that

- sufficient detail is present about the current ordering and tracking process
- terminology has been generalized to cover decomposition
- "forced arrows" have been added to the modified parent diagram

A typical correction is to add boundary arrows to the parent diagram, since the modeling of the detail should uncover additional use of data that was not obvious from the more general, parent diagram. These are called "forced arrows," since the decomposition of the parent box forces the arrows to be added to the parent. Actually, instead of forcing additional arrows, we may be able to include the new data in one of the existing pipelines. This potential is considered first to reduce the amount of clutter that we add to the model.

We are not yet ready to release the diagrams as a reader kit. First, a quick completeness and correctness check is made by running events through the diagrams to see if they represent a reasonable story. This may cause additional arrows to be added or names on the boxes or arrows to be changed.

Step 6: Run Scenarios

✔ Walk through the diagram for selected events

✔ Check all what-if possibilities

✔ Make sure all activities have controls and outputs

Figure E-22: Step 6, Run Scenarios.

Finally, we must ensure that the rules of IDEF0 have been obeyed. Some common software tools include this type of automated check, but we will perform a manual check here. One of the most common corrections involves adding control arrows to boxes that have none. (Recall that each box must have at least one control arrow—a requirement of the rules of IDEF0.) If an activity has no control arrow, we must consider: What controls how this activity works? Does it follow a schedule? Are there company manuals that dictate how it works? Is there a government standard with which it must comply? Did the previous processes result in any data that have a controlling influence on this activity? Are there any human factors that control the activity? The addition of arrows as a result of this scrutiny may then result in additional forced arrows that either must be made compatible with the parent activity's arrow structure or must be set aside.

We are finally ready for a reader/author review cycle, a kind of walkthrough session. (See Figure E-23.)

Step 7: Run the Reader/Author Cycle

✔ Select as first reader another author who should be instructed to

- catch remaining mistakes and omissions

- provide in-depth commentary on the breakdown

✔ Select experts for the second round

✔ Select other involved people for the final round, including

- management in the approval chain

- staff impacted by the diagrammed process

Figure E-23: Step 7, Run the Reader/Author Cycle.

This step first involves either making a reader kit or instructing the software tool to create one automatically. The kit is sent to the set of readers determined by the current review status of the diagrams. If this is the first review (that is, if the diagram is brand-new), then it is usually wise to send the kit to a single reader who is an experienced IDEF0 author. Limiting the review to a single reader helps avoid having several readers all catching obvious errors and embarrassing the author. Later reader cycles move up the management hierarchy until the information is the best that the entire group can identify.

This Appendix, through use of the Ben's Burgers case study and the seven steps of the modeling process, provides a brief overview of what can often be a deeply complex analysis of an enterprise, an analysis process that thanks to IDEF0 will almost always be successful.

KEY TERMS

The terms defined here are basic to the understanding of the method used throughout this book. This listing is not intended to be a complete glossary of all terms used.

Activity/Process/Function   An *activity* is the smallest of the three forms of happening—something that is an action, rather than a static thing. A *process* is a group of activities joined together to accomplish a major task (the design process, the painting process, the planning process). A *function* is a role that occurs many times in the sequence of running an enterprise and requires a particular training or expertise associated with it (the management function, the training function, the quality assurance function). These three terms have specific meanings to various people. For the purposes of this book, any one of these words may be used for a happening.

A-0 diagram   The top-most diagram in an IDEF0 model. Pronounced "a minus zero."

Arrow   A directed container for the things (as opposed to the happenings) that comprise the contents of an IDEF0 model. An arrow on an IDEF0 diagram may show the interface between two boxes on the diagram (an internal arrow), or it may be a boundary arrow (an interface to an activity on the parent diagram). An arrow may contain anything that has no action associated with it: discrete objects, people, systems, information, and so forth. The term "data

207

arrow" is typically used to speak about an IDEF0 arrow, but the word "data" does not imply a restriction to information only. An arrow may include such esoteric items as "satisfaction," items that are used up (like parts of an assembly), continuously available things (like electricity or temperature readings), or any other item that is static and may serve as an input, control, output, or mechanism in the model.

AS-IS The name for the IDEF0 model that shows how an enterprise now operates, as opposed to a TO-BE model, which shows how the enterprise will operate in the future (after changes are implemented).

Author A person who has been trained in the creation of IDEF0 models. He may also be a reader, but the label *author* is reserved for a person who is not only trained in how to read the IDEF0 diagrams but is able to create diagrams and models himself.

Boundary arrow An arrow showing one of its ends (head or tail) unconnected on the diagram. It is therefore an inter-diagram interface. Boundary arrows either show an *ICOM* to indicate the precise connection to the parent diagram, or show a tunnel (parentheses) to indicate that there is no connection to the parent.

Box A rectangle identifying an IDEF0 activity. The box contains a verb phrase naming the activity. The box name is merely a placeholder for the decomposition diagram for that activity. Therefore, all activities are contained in the bottom-most boxes (not the decomposed boxes of the model structure).

Bundling The process of combining several arrows into a common "pipeline" or conduit. The bundling of arrows on an IDEF0 diagram is intended to match the arrows' level of detail to that of the boxes.

Business process reengineering An approach to analyzing and restructuring the processes of an enterprise.

Child The decomposition of an activity box in an IDEF0 model is typically called the activity's "child" diagram. The parent of the diagram is the activity box that was decomposed to generate the child diagram.

Clustering The process of combining several related activities into a more general activity. It is typically employed when the number of identified activities must be reduced to obey the "six or fewer" rule of IDEF0, that no diagram may have more than six boxes.

Decomposition The original form of breakdown used to create a top-down function model in SADT and IDEF0. The process of decomposing an activity is to define the sub-activities without regard for the timing or the context of the activity. Other forms of breakdown include applying the activity at different points in time (for example, wash before bed or wash in the morning) or showing how the parent activity is used in different environments (for example, wash the car, wash the dishes, or wash the dog).

DoD The Department of Defense of the United States. The DoD policy committee adopted IDEF0 and IDEF1X as the standard methods to be used with their reengineering efforts in downsizing or reinventing their portion of the government.

DRE A detailed reference expression is a shorthand text used to point to a specific location on a diagram in a model. A specific arrow head or tail, or one branch of an arrow with forks and joins, may be identified using a DRE. The DRE is also written outside and below the right-hand corner of an IDEF0 box to indicate that a decomposition of that box exists, and to identify the C-number of that decomposition diagram. Another use of the DRE comes in conjunction with tunneled arrows, where the boundary arrow on a diagram does not connect to its parent diagram, but occurs elsewhere in the model. The DRE is used to identify the spot (source or target) of such a boundary arrow.

Enterprise A company, a group of companies, or a coalition (industry, commercial, university, or government) organized together to accomplish a goal, a kind of system. In the Department of Defense, an enterprise might be the Army or the Navy, or a strike force assembled to meet a threat (for example, the Gulf War or the Somalia force).

Enterprise analysis As defined by the Department of Transportation in a request for proposal: "The study of an enterprise to define its activities or functions; how the various functions performed in the enterprise are distributed and conducted; and the competitive, regulatory, and technical environment of the enterprise."

External arrow   A boundary arrow that occurs on the top-most (A-0) diagram in an IDEF0 model. An external arrow represents an interface between the model and its environment (things and happenings outside the model's scope).

FEO   A for-exposition-only diagram is used by an author to convey an important point, but the FEO is not considered to be part of the formal IDEF0 model. The purpose of an FEO is to expose some information about the diagram, such as the source and target of a specific arrow in the model. An FEO diagram is drawn on the same diagram form as a basic IDEF0 diagram, and it is cross-referenced to its related IDEF0 diagram through the "Used At" box in the upper-left corner of the diagram form.

ICOM   Stands for input, control, output, and mechanism, the four sides of a box on an IDEF0 diagram. An ICOM is an off-page connector of the form "C2" or "O1" (control number 2 or output number 1), and is used to link the arrow structure between IDEF0 diagrams. Many computer support tools automatically generate ICOMs when decomposing an activity box, to remind the author that a connection is required to make the new diagram fit properly into the model structure. Through common practice, the term ICOM has come to mean any arrow on an IDEF0 diagram, but it is not used as such in this book.

IDEF1X modeling method   An entity-attribute-relationship method of modeling the information structure of a topic. Typically used to analyze the information of an enterprise and to lay the foundation for building an integrated database on a computer.

Migration model   Depicts the process of changing the enterprise to implement the reengineering recommendations—the dynamics of changing the enterprise from the AS-IS to the TO-BE condition.

Parent diagram   The diagram one level of detail above the decomposition diagram. The parent is the diagram on which the decomposed activity box appears.

Purpose of a model   Defines why the model is developed. The purpose statement appears on the top-most diagram in the model structure (the A-0 diagram), and is typically in the form of the statement "This model will be used to . . ." The purpose is defined at the outset of an IDEF0 modeling effort.

Reader A person who has been trained in the syntax and semantics of IDEF0, and who is capable of examining an IDEF0 model and understanding its content. A reader may or may not be trained in the creation of models.

Scope of the model The subject matter that is covered by the model. The scope includes the starting and stopping point, as well as the type of subject matter covered. For example, a model of product development may or may not include the point at which it is conceptualized, or it may be restricted to the manufacturing of the product only. The end of the model may include delivery to the customer, or it may go all the way through the maintenance and after-sale customer support. Also, the scope may or may not include the development of its documentation or be restricted to the manufacturing of the physical product only. The model scope is defined at the start of a new IDEF0 modeling effort.

System Any combination of interacting elements organized to produce a desired end result. The elements may be people, procedures, information, resources, raw materials, machinery, tools, activities, functions, processes, and so on. The result may be a service or a product. The system may be a company, an enterprise or coalition made up of many companies, or a portion of a company, such as a division or a product group. For the model of a system to be useful, the modeling method must depict all of its elements, including all factors needed to control it, plan its future development, or manage its change.

Text Material that accompanies a completed IDEF0 model and is used to highlight features of the diagram. The text may employ DREs that point to specific items on the diagram.

TO-BE An IDEF0 model that depicts the operation of the enterprise after the changes resulting from the reengineering effort are implemented.

Viewpoint The perspective used when emphasizing or deemphasizing aspects of a topic, such as whether an item should be included in the model or how highly it should be placed (the higher in the model structure, the more emphasis). A viewpoint typically represents a group of people with a common background and education (a common "culture") in an enterprise, such as personnel in financial, quality assurance, sales, computer software, or management areas. A single viewpoint should be taken for an entire model. Models from other viewpoints may be developed separately and then linked to each other using DRE expressions. Mixing viewpoints on a single model typically obscures the model's communication ability.

INDEX

Accounting system examples, 25–27, 37–38
Activity, 56, 83–84
    See also Box; Breakdowns
    clusters, 188–90, 208–9
    defined, 207
    layout of, 86, 191
    list, 86, 187–90
    maximum number of, 9, 86, 115–16
    naming convention, 110
    quality of, 123
    rules for, 107–10
Activity-based costing (ABC) approach, 52, 185
Aerospace industry, 4, 5, 17
Air Force
    AFCAM program, 5, 6, 172
    computer-aided manufacturing and, 5
    ICAM program and, 10, 17
    IDEF0 and, 7, 17
    ManTech Office, 4, 5, 7, 173
    modeling method, 7
Air Force Computer-Aided Manufacturing (AFCAM) program, 5, 6, 172
Approval levels
    draft, 84, 101
    publication, 84, 101, 102, 104

    recommended, 101, 102, 134
    working, 84, 101, 103
Arrow, 2, 12, 55, 56, 57, 58, 86–87, 207
    See also Boundary arrow; Call arrow; Control arrow; IDEF0 rules; Input arrow; Mechanism arrow; Output arrow
    branches, 58, 72, 114
    bundling, 98, 107, 129–31, 134, 193, 208
    content, 56, 57, 98–99, 114, 116
    data interface, 30
    defined, 207
    external, 210
    flow restriction rule, 114
    fog factor and, 124
    forced, 203
    forks, 59, 62, 87
    joins, 59, 62, 87
    labeling, 56, 57, 87–88, 107, 113, 124–26, 130, 131, 135
    layout rules, 87
    parentheses and, 112
    pathways, 86, 87
    pipeline, 59, 88, 203
    plug-compatibility, 110–12
    purpose of, 133, 134